Endorsements

Rev. Courtney Clayton Jenkins has penned what I wish someone had told me 35 years ago. Her thoughtful and experienced-based insights, and her desire to help other women in ministry have motivated her to offer meaningful and practical steps to living fruitfully, healthily and faithfully, while making a difference in the world. Life is filled with ups and downs, but this book reminds us that wisdom is the key to sanity and stability.

—Rev. Dr. Elaine M. Flake
Greater Allen A.M.E. Cathedral of New York
Jamaica, New York

Rev. Courtney Clayton Jenkins takes women in ministry firmly by the "neck" with her book. She touches "right now" concerns that we keep ignoring every day. She lovingly forces us to see what we are doing to ourselves. I truly recommend this devotional gift. Thank you Precious Woman of God for making our futures longer and better. This book belongs in our hands. I am "stepping back and "stepping up"! This time for real!

—Rev. Dr. Wilma R. Johnson
New Prospect Missionary Baptist Church
Detroit, Michigan

Rev. Courtney Clayton Jenkins, in *Stepping Back to Step Up*, offers her energetic yet seeking respite, youthful yet wise, passionate yet joyous, and experienced yet still journeying voice to the deeply needed, yet often lacking, self-care resources for women in pastoral leadership grounded in the biblical text. The six-week refresher course is designed to insure women in leadership put away their capes, tights and bionic energy supply to "step back", reassess, refuel, renegotiate and reenergize as they "step up" to live out the multifaceted call on their lives. This is a welcomed, manageable and spiritual offering for women in any profession.

—Dr. Teresa L. Fry Brown
Bandy Professor of Preaching, Candler School of Theology at Emory University
Atlanta, Georgia

For women in ministry, it is often hard to know when life is out of balance. The busyness of our lives causes us to neglect the warning signals that we need to take a minute to reset. Often we think we are running on fuel when in fact we are running on fumes. It is not until there is a mental drain or health challenge that we realize that something has gone wrong. Who better to help busy women gain a wholesome, spiritual perspective on what it means to be the best that God has called us to be —while at the same time being all that God has called us to be – than a woman who is herself very busy. As wife, mother, Pastor, preacher, sister and friend Rev. Courtney Clayton Jenkins wears many hats and juggles many responsibilities in the hectic and often chaotic world of pastoral ministry. In the unique position of both being a pastor and being married to a pastor, she has the added responsibility of sharing professional stories across the dining room table. In *Step Back to Step Up* she focuses with the heart and compassion of a pastor, realistically and candidly, on how to handle the challenges of being a woman in ministry. Using scripture and anecdotal commentary as a guide, we are challenged to take just 10 minutes, five days per week to bring a sense of calm centering to our mind, body and spirit. In just enough time (10 minutes) to catch our breath, we are given an excellent strategy that will bring balance and vision to our day and our life. Women who are serious about holistic ministry for the long haul will want to have this valuable resource in their home, car and office or any place where they can take ten minutes to "step back to step up!"

—Carolyn Ann Knight
Preacher, Professor, Social Justice Advocate
Smyrna, Georgia

Creative! Insightful reflections! Powerful scriptures! Reflections that minister to the spiritual core of a woman in ministry! Questions that challenge! Transformational reading! This meditation book encompasses all of these descriptive phrases and more. A must read for those who have come to the place of knowing "stepping back to step up is not an option.

—Rev. Dr. Jessica Kendall Ingram
Episcopal Supervisor
First Episcopal District African Methodist Episcopal Church
Philadelphia, PA

Rev. Courtney Clayton Jenkins is a pastor, preacher, wife, mother, visionary and community leader who knows what it is like to wear many hats. With the heart of a pastor and the skill of a life coach, Rev. Courtney has tapped into the wellspring of life for all who desire to balance life, love, leadership, work and rest for effective ministry. Women in ministry will find this devotional a useful and inspiring resource for nurturing the spirit and the soul.

—Dr. Gina M. Stewart, Senior Pastor
Christ Missionary Baptist Church
Memphis, Tennessee

Rev. Courtney Clayton Jenkins has pulled back the covers that women in ministry cling to so desperately, pretending that all is well with our souls, relationships and ministries. The truth is most of us are over-extended, overworked, disconnected and under-appreciated. She invites us on an adventure to name our stresses and to claim our blessings. Rev. Jenkins understands the call to ministry and the call to self-care. Using her own ministry and life as a foundation, she gives us the opportunity to try some new things on our journey. Jam-packed with wisdom, insight, humor and inspiration, this devotional encourages women to connect more fully with God, with other women in ministry and leadership, and with ourselves. Her practical, logical, and –dare I say – fun Action Steps along with short devotionals allow even the busiest among us to commune with God, Jesus and the Holy Spirit each day. The payoff: renewed relationships, new energy for ministry and leadership, and rest for our weary souls. I challenge you to take on this six-week spiritual boot camp; dare to "step back, so you can step up" to all that God is calling you to be and do, as women and as leaders. Rev. Courtney Clayton Jenkins shows us the way!

—Rev. Barbara J. Essex
Author, *Bad Girls of the Bible: Exploring Women of Questionable Virtue*
Cleveland, Ohio

What a timely and necessary work! Caregivers also need care. Thank you Rev. Courtney Clayton Jenkins for reminding female clergy that we MUST maintain balance: spirit, soul and body. Our state of being impacts our ministry. Great job!

—Dr. Karen Bethea
Set the Captives Free Outreach Center
Windsor Mill, Maryland

Rev. Courtney Clayton Jenkins is a phenomenal teacher, preacher and pastor. Her personal challenges and experiences lend credence to this devotional penned to assist women in ministry with balance, excellence and a strategy for perseverance.

—Reverend Dr. Sabrina J. Ellis
Pentecostal Church of Christ
Cleveland, Ohio

Whether feeding the multitudes, preaching in the synagogues, teaching on the mountains and healing all manner of sickness and disease, Jesus retreated regularly, sending the people away, or disappearing without a warning to a place of rest and peace. Rev. Courtney Clayton Jenkins builds upon this principle of balance in her book, *Stepping Back to Step Up* I am a woman in ministry who has been married 22 years, raising children while pursuing personal dreams and aspirations; therefore, I know firsthand how important balance is to the lives of women in ministry. I look forward to being spiritually, physically, mentally and emotionally renewed as I apply Courtney's five-fold devotional concept to my life and ministry.

—Rev. Dr. Antoinette G. Alvarado
Grace Church International
Atlanta, Georgia

The old saying goes, "If you want to get something done, give it to a busy person" – and *busy* is the operative word in most of our lives today. But the effects of the busyness of our lives as women clergy has caused some of us to question the efficacy of this old maxim. *Stepping Back to Step Up* is just what clergy who juggle family, ministry and life need to properly balance, focus and be equipped for the demands that lie ahead. Rev. Courtney Clayton Jenkins is the epitome of a busy and committed *but* balanced and effective pastor. We would all do well to incorporate these sacred, life-giving 10-minute devotions into our *busy* daily lives!

—Rev. LeQuita H. Porter, Pastor,
East Preston United Baptist Church of Nova Scotia
East Preston, Nova Scotia

Each page of this book offers a sacred space of refreshment and encouragement for women who have dedicated their lives serving in professional ministry. Thank you Rev. Courtney Clayton Jenkins for answering God's call to offer words of life and hope to other women who have answered God's call to offer words of life and hope!

—Rev. Lisa D Jenkins
St. Matthew's Baptist Church of Harlem
State Coordinator, Women in Ministry, Empire Baptist Missionary Convention

As a pastor who's wise beyond her years, Rev. Courtney Clayton Jenkins reminds us of the necessity of self-care. She challenges us to take a step back and intentionally learn how to minister to ourselves while discovering how to be spiritually present in our own lives. This book should be a requirement for all female pastors.

—Rev. Babydoll Kennedy
Burks Chapel AME Church
Paducah, KY

Finally, a devotional book geared specifically to women in ministry! If you need a devotional book that speaks directly to your heart, soul and mind and one that convicts, encourages and empowers, this book is it. Just 10 minutes a day for a reawakening!

—Pastor Michele Humphrey
Imani United Church of Christ
Cleveland, Ohio

This daily devotional is exactly what God would order for us all. As a woman "thrust into not just a role of pastoral leading - but also juggling a myriad of responsibilities," I will return to this book and practice regularly over the course of my life.

—The Reverend Cheryle R.C. Hanna, DMin.
Fourth Avenue Baptist Church
Ottawa, Ontario, Canada

Rev Courtney Clayton Jenkins has allowed God to transform her experiences into a well of healing water that revives, empowers and affirms. Lower your bucket and get your fill of balance, excellence, vision, strategy and perseverance so you can be the leader God has called you to be.

—Rev. Sheri D. Smith Clayborn
St. John African Methodist Episcopal Church
Huntsville, AL

Juggling the leadership responsibilities of ministry, Motherhood, Marriage and Me can often be overwhelming and exhausting! Rev. Courtney Clayton Jenkins' Stepping back to Step Up devotion is a breath of fresh air as it encourages women leaders to pump the breaks and find daily rest in God in order to be recharged for all that one is called to do!

—Rev. Dr. Stacey Edwards-Dunn
Executive Minister of Community
Engagement/Transformation
Trinity United Church of Christ
Founder of Fertility for Colored Girls

Stepping Back to Step Up

A Six-Week Devotional to
Recharge, Refresh, and Refuel Women in Ministry

COURTNEY CLAYTON JENKINS

Team Jenkins Press

CLEVELAND

Edited by: Katara Patton

Interior Design: Sarco Press Book Design

Cover Art: Shanequa Gay

Cover Design: Shanequa Gay

Author Photo: McKinley Wiley

ISBN-13: 978-0692512531 (Team Jenkins)

ISBN-10: 0692512535

In Memory

In memory of Ms. Lucille Kiser, who entered my life encouraging me to always *step back*.

Dedication

For Cory, who has always stood by my side encouraging me to *step up.*

Acknowledgments

I am indebted to God for all those who have given so generously of their time and energies to make this book possible. To the team that has supported me in pushing this vision to reality, thank you. To Rev. Dr. Cynthia L. Hale for lending your name to this work and for your wise counsel through the years, I am deeply appreciative. To the members – and especially the staff – of South Euclid United Church of Christ for walking with me as I seek to fulfill the calling on my life, I am so grateful.

When you're at the edge of a cliff,
sometimes progress is a step backwards.
– African Proverb

Foreword

*L*IFE IS DEMANDING FOR ANYONE. But when you add ministry to it, life can sometimes be overwhelming, especially for us as women. There are so many people and responsibilities that claim our time and attention. We are expected to be all things to all people and fulfill so many roles. We are expected to be preacher, teacher, visionary leader, pastor, worship leader, prophetess, evangelist, counselor, social change agent, responsible parent, loving and supportive spouse, secretary, bookkeeper, organizer and whatever else anyone thinks he or she needs from us.

For all of us, even as single women, there is this need to find balance. While it is important for us to fulfill our responsibilities as pastor or minister with excellence, and serve the needs of others with love, it is equally important for us to be healthy and happy in the execution of our ministries and in life.

Too often, we think we have to meet the needs of others and ensure their well-being at the expense of our own. Perhaps, like me, you have been told that **Joy** is **Jesus, Others, You,** which suggests that Jesus comes first, others second and you and your needs should be considered last.

But, Jesus said in Matthew 22:34-39 in response to the expert in the law who approached him with the question, "Teacher, what is the greatest commandment in the Law?" that you are to "Love the Lord your God with all your heart, soul and mind. This is the greatest commandment. And then you are to love your neighbors as you love yourself." We cannot love, serve or respond to the needs of others until we have met our own needs.

This speaks to balance. Finding balance in one's life is learning to appropriately handle all the relationships and responsibilities that are an essential part of life and ministry while at the same time, insuring that you are healthy and whole.

How does one achieve balance in one's life? Well, it's quite simple. I learned early in my life and career the importance of what I call, "an early morning rendezvous with God." Now, most of you would just call this morning devotions. And it is! I called it a rendezvous because, as a single woman, the term was sexy. I needed to know that there was a man who wanted to have a special and private meeting with me.

Seriously, I used the term because a rendezvous is a meeting at an appointed place and time. To have a rendezvous with someone is not to leave the meeting to chance. It's setting a date, a time, a place to meet, and it's keeping the appointment, whatever the cost.

Devotions or a time with God daily should not be left to chance. Devotions should be a daily habit, at a certain time and place, so that it becomes a holy habit, one that you cannot live without.

I find my time with God critical to life and ministry for several reasons. First of all, it is important for nurturing my intimate and personal relationship with my Savior and the lover of my soul.

Nurturing any relationship takes time and undivided attention and that is no less true of my relationship with God.

Secondly, a time with God first thing in the morning helps determine my attitude, my agenda and my effectiveness throughout the day. During my time of communion and conversation with God, I share my hopes and dreams, my concerns and challenges for the day and ask for his direction, strength and confidence. During our time, God gives me everything I need for a successful day.

Through the years, God has revealed His vision for my life, the church, or some other project that I am working on. It is during my devotions that God has revealed everything I have needed to develop the Ray of Hope Christian Church into the ministry that it currently is.

God also makes me aware of those people and situations that I will encounter during the day and gives me the wisdom to handle every situation effectively and graciously. Now whether I use the wisdom God gives me is another matter.

Thirdly, it is during my intimate moments with God that I have learned to love and take care of myself. One time in particular, I was struggling with feelings of inadequacy for ministry and feeling overwhelmed by it all. God reminded me that I am fearfully and wonderfully made, fully equipped for the ministry to which He has called me.

It was in that moment that I was also reminded that I needed to "come apart before I came apart." I was so frazzled because I was tired and needed rest. Needless to say, I take seriously my personal and private time of rest, rejuvenation and renewal.

There is nothing more important to me than my daily rendezvous with God. I have to fight for it because there are so many distractions, so many demands that seem in the moment much more important. When I allow those distractions and demands to override my time with God, I pay dearly for it.

I am so glad that Rev. Courtney Clayton Jenkins has given us this resource. I always need a sweet reminder of the importance of "Stepping Back to Step Up." Jesus said it and it is true. "Seek first the Kingdom of God and His righteousness and all things will be given to you."

Cynthia L. Hale, B.S. M.Div., DMin.
Senior Pastor
Ray of Hope Christian Church
(Disciples of Christ)

Contents

Introduction

INISTRY AND LEADERSHIP. This is hard work to which we have been called. It requires so much. We are up to the task—most of the time. Yet, in the midst of family and professional demands, when is there time to do what we need to do in order to keep ourselves healthy, whole, energized, and focused?

In other words, who takes care of the pastor? Who helps the leader take time for personal devotions and prayer? How can I step back, in order to be able to step up? Women in ministry are busy. We put forth the vision for our congregations; set the spiritual tone for those who follow our leadership; call the meetings; plan for worship; assist in faith formation; and put out the fires that happen at the most inconvenient times. We hold it all together-- together for home, together for church, together for extended family, together for community. It can all be too much, and yet, this is God's call on our lives.

For those of us who are also wives and mothers—well, it is easy to put ourselves absolutely last on those to-do lists. We simply don't have enough time—we are so busy doing for everyone else that there is virtually no time to just be. Single or married, we often shortchange ourselves and go without proper self-care. Then we are exhausted, depressed, angry, and beaten down. We struggle with the motivation to complete the task.

It is absolutely imperative that we create space to pray and reflect on our service, our leadership, and our lives. We cannot keep hectic schedules and move at a frenetic pace without soon crashing and burning out. I know from personal experience. We know we should slow down—if not to smell the roses, then certainly to rest and rejuvenate. I have found that, when we do slow down, even if for a few minutes, we are better because of it. When we don't slow down and breathe, we are ineffective and scattered all over the place.

Slowing down is just what we intend to do for the next six weeks. If you can't stop for a little while, at least slow it down. I challenge you to spend just ten minutes with God and yourself every day— before you walk out the door of your home, before you enter that first meeting of the day, before you rush in to take care of all those things waiting for you—just ten minutes to hear the Holy Spirit speak to you. Perhaps you take ten minutes early in the morning before your home begins its hustle and bustle. Or when you first arrive at your desk, with a cup of coffee in hand, be determined that you will not answer the phone for those ten minutes and that you will be still and know that God is with you that day. Take the time to read this devotional while getting a pedicure. Breathe and meditate at lunch time. Take it all in at the end of the day. Make the time within your day for you to become a better you and a more effective leader.

I believe these ten minutes can change your life and your ministry for the better. With these sacred minutes set aside, I believe renewed energy and strength for the journey will be yours. Yes, there are other resources that nurture our spirits, and they require hours we just don't have on a regular basis. There are plenty of other resources out there, but rarely are they made for women who are in the thick of balancing it all. Yes, we read, study, reflect, and meditate—in preparing sermons, in setting meeting agendas, as support for visiting the sick and shut-in. But we rip and run so much, we don't even notice our tanks are on empty until our very being is stranded on the side of the road and others are passing us by. It just might be time to step back so that we can step up.

This devotional is designed to be read Monday through Friday; there are no devotionals for Saturdays or Sundays. There are five areas of emphasis:

• Balance on Mondays – We must strive to be effective at home and in our ministries. Balance is about how to prioritize our lives so there is room for all the responsibilities and demands and room for us to take care of ourselves. It is not selfish to be concerned about our own health and well-being. Our lives depend on balance.

• Excellence on Tuesdays – We must strive to give our best—to family, to church, and to ourselves. Too many times we give half-hearted efforts, or we don't allot enough time to do the work that is required of us. We must set our priorities so that we are always at our best; we are not called to be perfect, but we are called to excellence. Why would we shortchange the God who gave and continues to give us the best?

• Vision on Wednesdays – No ministry is sustainable without a vision; no life is well-lived without a vision. The vision helps us get up each day to do the work and keeps us focused. The more attention we give to the vision, the more energized our lives are.

•   Strategy on Thursdays – Vision without strategy is merely a dream. We must have a plan, and we must work that plan. Strategy is about calling on all the resources needed to make a vision a reality—in our personal lives and in our ministries.

•   Perseverance on Fridays: Balance, excellence, vision, and strategy require energy; we can be tempted to give up, but that is not what our calling is all about. What do we need to keep on keeping on when we are tired, discouraged, or disappointed?

Each devotional includes an Action Step—one thing we can do to embody the theme for that day. Some Action Steps are one-time events; others will take some time. The point is that we practice what we are learning. So, let's begin each day inspired, motivated, and edified for the work of leadership that is our life, calling, and mission.

Let's step back so that we can step up!

Day: 1

My First Church Is at Home

*That is why a man leaves his father and mother and
is united to his wife, and they become one flesh.*

--Genesis 2:24

TOO MANY HATS! My wife hat. My mommy hat. My pastor hat. My daughter hat. My sister hat. My girlfriend hat. If I am honest about it, I sometimes let the pastor hat take over all of my other responsibilities. It is not something I am proud of, I confess.

I am compelled by the vision God has given me for my family and this call to ministry. Sometimes, though, that call takes over everything. It consumes all. Late nights. Early mornings. Going non-stop. Unhealthy eating habits. Naps at night so I can get up to finish a sermon or prep for a meeting. Cutting it close and sometimes running late. I am famous for working through my lunch at my desk, unless, of course, it's a lunch-time meeting. Even then, my objective is to bring forth this vision God has given me for this ministry. If I am not careful and if I do not pay close attention, I can easily lose all sense of how all-consuming ministry can become. Of course, all of this is magnified by the fact that I find ministry to be fun and exciting. I love what I am called to do.

At the same time, I've learned that, in order for me to do ministry effectively, I actually need to do a better job of balancing my other hats. Too often in ministry, we focus so much on the work that we neglect self and family. We take for granted the people and places that keep us grounded and that renew us when life gets to be too much. In truth, it's the hats of my family roles that really keep me warm at night! I should not neglect them.

Do you suffer with "five more minutes?" Sadly, I do. All you ask of others is just "five more minutes" of time to work on the sermon, to prep for the meeting, to get dinner together. Yet, it's never really five more minutes. Five minutes is really fifteen minutes or forty-five minutes. When this happens, it begs us to ask the question, am I wearing my hats properly? In truth, most of us are overworked and we justify our imbalance by saying, "It's because I am doing the Lord's work." Has God called us to do the work of ministry at the neglect of ourselves or our families? I don't think so.

My husband and I often use this expression: "My first church is at home" to describe how we prioritize family, church, and other ministry opportunities. I've seen too many people in ministry who have made the church first, not God, and they have paid an extremely high price. While their public ministries prospered, their private lives suffered because they put more time into church than into their own flesh and blood. I don't think God honors our putting off of family. I believe what God honors is when we make our family first. God honors us when we honor the covenant we have made with those whom we care for and love.

It was during our pre-marital counseling session that we were told, "Don't have an affair with ministry." If we are honest, it is easier said than done! For many of us, single or married, ministry is our mistress. It feeds us, it loves on us, it builds us up; but it does not keep us warm at night. Ministry doesn't care for us when we are sick. Ministry may even disappoint us in the end. This unhealthy imbalance has to stop.

I will never forget a mentor of mine saying to Cory and me, "Never forsake your family for a church you will one day retire from." I am of the mindset that if my home is not "right," then church can't be "right" either. Before we put another hat on our head, let's take a good long look in the mirror and find the hats that matter. To do this properly, we must begin by removing all the hats from our head and taking a moment to simply let our hair down. Perhaps some hats need to be removed permanently. Other hats may need to be cleaned or cleared for a season. All our hats need prioritizing. I don't want my neck to break because I keep piling on the hats.

Good leaders know how to ensure that family remains first and that ministry is not all-consuming. We must put just as much time, energy, and effort into making sure things are right at home first. Remember, the Church as we know it began in homes, long before church buildings were erected. We must learn to set healthy boundaries on a daily basis. Isn't it time you honor your day off? Isn't it time we enjoy the company of a loved one without our minds becoming consumed with our to-do list? You and I can't be "on" all the time. We must be more intentional.

Step Back: What is one thing you can do today to let those who make up your familial support system know that you appreciate them? How can you bless a colleague who has been there for you or a friend who has supported you? Do it today!

Balance

Day: 2

I'm Every Woman

Then God said, "Let us make mankind in our
image, in our likeness, so that they may rule over
the fish in the sea and the birds in the sky, over the
livestock and all the wild animals, and over all the
creatures that move along the ground."
So God created mankind in his own image, in the
image of God he created them; male and female he
created them.
God blessed them and said to them, "Be fruitful
and increase in number; fill the earth and subdue
it. Rule over the fish in the sea and the birds in the
sky and over every living creature that moves on the
ground."

--Genesis 1:26-28

OD CREATED US FEMALE—in God's own image and likeness. God had a plan in mind when we were created. Women are the crescendo of creation. God intentionally made us the way we are, and we are no mistake. We embody the attributes of God: We are creative, adventurous, loving, caring, and compassionate, among others. Beyond the attributes of God, there is the gifting God has placed within us: preaching, teaching, administration, serving, encouraging, leadership, giving, mercy, wisdom, and so much more.

Isn't it time to reassess your gifts and give God praise for the many ways that God has endowed you with the power to do great things? When you think of the way God has uniquely put your gifts together so that you might serve in your vocation and reflect on the way God has gifted you for this calling to ministry, your soul should declare, "It is good." Not because we are perfect but because God intends to use our gifts all to his glory, in spite of us.

When we develop our gifts and we use them for the sake of the community, we are good stewards. Additionally, using our gifts with excellence demonstrates to those who follow our leadership how important it is to develop our gifts. How much more productive could our churches be if everyone was developing his or her spiritual gifts? We can't expect excellent, gifts-based ministry in others if we don't demonstrate it within ourselves.

More than a decade ago, Anders Ericsson and his colleagues at Berlin's elite Academy of Music did a study with musicians. With the help of professors, they divided violinists into three groups: world-class soloists, good violinists, and those who were unlikely to play professionally. All of them started playing around the same age, and they practiced about the same amount of time until the age of eight. Research indicated that at age eight, practice habits diverged. The research found that by the age of twenty, the average players had logged about 4,000 hours of practice time; the good violinists totaled about 8,000 hours of practice; and the elite performers, the crème de la crème, set the standard with 10,000 hours of logged practice time.

Yes, we are gifted even though we are flawed. Yet, to magnify the gifts God has given us to the glory of God, there is no denying that our gifts are refined over time. When it comes to developing your gifts, intentionality is key. While there may be other gifts you feel might be more effective in this season of ministry, show God how faithful you are by developing the gifts you already have. God created us and called us just as we are. We don't have to justify our existence or our right to answer God's call. Yet, we glorify God in awesome ways when we develop our gifts.

As women in ministry, we do not have to imitate men. I've seen women taking the gifts God has given them to imitate our male colleagues. I've also seen women trying to dress like, act like, or even look like a more seasoned woman in ministry. This must stop. The gifts God has given you were not designed to be counterfeit. The gifts God has given you are authentic. Authenticity cannot be imitated.

We are called to be ministers and leaders. We should embrace who we are as women in ministry and allow God to work through our feminine ways and perspectives. You serve best when you are you! For when you allow the gifts of God to be fully demonstrated in your life, God is glorified, and we are most effective.

Step Back: When was the last time you took a Spiritual Gifts Assessment? Many of us took these early in our ministries. Now we assume we know our gifts. Find an online Spiritual Gifts Assessment, and see if your gifts are the same, or acknowledge how your gifts have changed in this season of ministry. Is there a new gift God has given you for this season to increase your effectiveness? Once you are clear about your gifts for this season of ministry, what steps will you take to enhance those gifts to assist you in securing success?

Wish List for Ministry

1. Develop & expand current properties for worship Center and Comm Outreach Cnt.

2. Dev + expand Parking Capasity

3. Devel. partnerships With other Churches to collaborate on Outreach efforts for, Healing, education and family services ... e.g. Women Support Groups, GED Prep + testing, Computer Programming etc...
——→

12

$\mathcal{D}ay: 3$

Imagination is Key

*The hand of the Lord was on me, and he brought
me out by the Spirit of the Lord and set me in the
middle of a valley; it was full of bones. He led me
back and forth among them, and I saw a great many
bones on the floor of the valley, bones that were
very dry. He asked me, "Son of man, can these
bones live?"
I said, "Sovereign Lord, you alone know."*

--Ezekiel 37:1-3

I DON'T QUITE BELIEVE ALL THE HYPE about dying churches. "Church" is a changing organism. We must evolve with it. Some churches are languishing, but many churches are alive and thriving. Those that are thriving probably have strong leadership and a clear vision they are working on daily to make a reality. We know, "Where there is no revelation, people cast off restraint" (Proverbs 29:18). I believe what is missing most from the twenty-first-century church is imagination when it comes to vision. We keep doing the same things over and over again. Subsequently, we are getting the same results; or no results.

Churches get stuck and use the "we've never done that before" mentality to define them. This phrase can be discouraging to a leader because people don't see what you see. If we let fear and stagnation guide us, we won't get anywhere. There is no good reason for death to be a part of the leadership equation. In fact, you ought to refuse such a mentality while you are serving in leadership.

God is not done with the world yet. Daily, God calls women to ministry. Daily, God shows those same women new mercies. Daily, God gives women in ministry the strength to see what others cannot. There has to be a purpose behind these callings, and daily, God is revealing this if we will look with open eyes.

What is the vision God has given to you? What has God shown you to be possible that others might say is impossible? What areas of ministry will be better because the Lord sent you that way? What work must be done under your leadership?

Ezekiel found himself facing a devastating situation—a valley of dried up bones. In the face of stark reality, God asked Ezekiel to imagine living, breathing people. God asked him to visualize what could be possible. I am sure there were parts of him that said it could not be so, but Ezekiel found a way for his "yes" to be louder than his "no."

You will have to do that, too, in order to see this vision become a reality. You will have to determine that the vision for new life is more powerful than the death that may be surrounding you. You will have to fix your eyes on the vision and turn your ears off to the naysayers.

I recall, early on in my pastorate, I decided to bring a children's choir from Uganda to my church. Many were scared and, as a result, apprehensive. The congregation was resistant and consumed with the cost. I knew, though, that this was what God wanted us to do. Many tried to change my mind, and others tried to scare me with thoughts of failure. What if we can't get all the funding? What if no one in the church wants to host children in their home? What if no one shows up? If I, as the leader, lost hope, then those who were willing to trust my vision would have given up hope, too. I stayed the course. I knew deep down that bringing that choir to my church was what the Lord wanted us to do.

I remember that night vividly. We had more than enough volunteers. We had raised over $7,000, and the house was packed with over 750 in attendance. In fact, that concert ended up unifying our church around the power of vision and faith. God showed me, and the vast majority of naysayers, what could be done. God did just what he said he would. Today, we must look into the reality of our ministry and leadership situation and see what others cannot. You are called to see it because you are the visionary leader assigned for this season of ministry. We need more women in leadership willing to imagine what is possible. Like the prophet Ezekiel, look beyond what is, and dream about what can be.

What will be a blessing? What will make Christ known in the earth? When is the last time you imagined something out of nothing? Do you believe this calling is for new life? New vision? New dreams? Well, it is! Our vision must be more than preaching to packed-out houses. If you are going to serve as a leader, you must have a clear vision for the ministry to which God is calling you! People follow leaders with vision. Rejoice in the call, and rejoice in a vision of what can be with God at the helm of our ship.

Step Back: Take five minutes to do this exercise. If time, money, church bullies, and resources were no objects, what would you do in your ministry or leadership setting? Be bold. Write it down and pray on it.

4. Violence prevention +
Community watch services
w/ local neighborhood
associations

5. Food distributions for
needy families

6. Parenting Training @
Frankford

7. Youth driven
initiatives

Our
Make Banner for ~~Church~~

Mission Statement.

Our
~~Doct~~ ~~Church~~ Declaration

Doctrinal Statement
(congated)

16

Day: 4

Blueprints in Hand

*"So make yourself an ark of cypress wood; make
rooms in it and coat it with pitch inside and out.
This is how you are to build it: The ark is to be
three hundred cubits long, fifty cubits wide and
thirty cubits high. Make a roof for it, leaving below
the roof an opening one cubit high all around. Put
a door in the side of the ark and make lower,
middle and upper decks."*

--Genesis 6:14-16

BUILDINGS DON'T JUST APPEAR BY MAGIC. Someone had a vision, and someone developed a plan to make that vision into a reality. The roadmap architects use to turn vision into reality is known as a blueprint. No building has ever been constructed without a blueprint. The blueprint tells us what goes where and how the building will be made and fortified.

God didn't leave the construction of the Ark solely up to Noah, nor did God leave the construction of the Temple all up to Solomon. God provided detailed instructions. Even during creation, God strategically ordered the days. God created with intentionality. We ought to do the same.

Beyond buildings and boats, in order for any vision to become reality, you must have a blueprint. What do you need for your vision to become reality? What will it cost you in time, energy, efforts, and resources? What materials should you use? How long will it take? Who are the best persons to get the job done? Who will get the permits? Who will vet the contractors? Who will be held accountable for ensuring we stay on budget and within a set timeframe?

As I am overseeing an 8.15 million dollar construction project for my church, I know the value of blueprints. In some cases, churches hire an architect to design or renovate a designated space; when those blueprints are taken to a contractor, the church officials may find out that, while the design looks beautiful, it cannot be built. This is because, while the architect had a great idea, the contractor knows that what has been envisioned may not be possible for any number of reasons. Therefore, The relationship between the architect and the contractor is imperative.

For example, I know of one church whose architect designed a beautiful new sanctuary. When the architect took the prints to the contractor, the contractor said, "The city will never approve this." The architect would not listen. He took the prints to the city, and the contractor was right. The city instructed the architect to go back and work with the contractor to come up with a design that was consistent with other neighborhood projects.

Many churches have a model of what their future church could look like sitting in their narthex. However, no steps have been taken to the turn the model into bricks and mortar except the establishment of a building fund.

In the case of my church, we are doing what is known as a "design–build." In this instance, the architect works alongside the contractor to ensure that the vision can become a reality. As we constructed our new space, we drew the blueprints with the future in mind, and the contractor was in the room to ensure it was all possible. At every meeting with the architect, the contractor was present. It made the difference.

At the time when we designed our nursery, there were no infants in our ministry. But we worked with the architect and the contractor to design a space that would hold ten cribs. The city had different regulations for rooms with five cribs versus those that held ten cribs. The architect helped us envision the room needs, but it was the contractor who ensured we were up to code to make the vision a reality. Today, that room is full of infants. The blueprint told us what steps to take, the contractor ensured it was up to code, and the ministry did the work to fill the room with infants.

Or another example is when we wired our building. Where should the telephones go? Do we want televisions in each classroom or some classrooms? How about computers and Internet? Where would the security alarms go? How would the heating and cooling be zoned? The blueprints served as a thorough guide that showed us exactly what the space was going to look like. It was not wise to develop the blueprints in isolation. The vision was made stronger by having the right people at the table as we drew up the blueprints and designed a space that the city would approve.

Isn't it time you and God engage in a design–build agreement? Let God do the designing. Let the Holy Spirit work within you to do the contracting. Ask God what people need to be at the table to bring the vision into reality.

The Bible declares that "iron sharpens iron" (Proverbs 27:17). In vision casting, the blueprint for the vision can be made stronger by inviting the right people to help see what you might miss. It's time to determine how the vision will become a reality.

Step Back: Begin to construct a vision board for your life and your ministry. On a poster board, make a collage of images, words, phrases, and sentences to illustrate the vision God has given you. Be specific and work on this over a period of time. When you are done, place the board someplace where you will see it regularly as a reminder that you are working toward that which God has shown you. If you already have a vision board, review it. Is that vision still what you see? What steps are you taking to move from vision to reality? Start taking action today!

Vision Board For Ministry:
1. Develop Community Partners
• Contact The Comm Assoc. President
• Contact The Local Catholic Church Leaders up the Street
• Contact Local Churches + Community Leaders
• Do introduction Cards + Go door to door to introduce yourself.

Day: 5

Get Up!

Do you not know?
Have you not heard?
The Lord is the everlasting God,
the Creator of the ends of the earth.
He will not grow tired or weary,
and his understanding no one can fathom.
He gives strength to the weary
and increases the power of the weak.
Even youths grow tired and weary,
and young men stumble and fall;
but those who hope in the Lord
will renew their strength.
They will soar on wings like eagles;
they will run and not grow weary,
they will walk and not be faint.

--Isaiah 40:28-31

I RECALL EARLY IN THE PASTORATE at my current church, lying in bed one morning, and I didn't want to get out of bed at all. I had been criticized and lied about. Members had talked about me on the telephone and in parking lots. Members had sent letters, anonymously, of course, to other members saying that I didn't have what it took to lead the congregation. On top of that, there were more meetings scheduled than I cared to attend, I needed to plan for Sunday worship, and I

21

had just put out a fire that had been brewing in another part of the ministry.

The task just seemed like too much weight to bear. Why press on another day in the ministry when I could stay in that nice, warm bed, pull the covers over my head, and sleep through the pain and the fatigue. For goodness sakes, there was a Law & Order marathon on the television. I felt like I could just stay in that bed forever.

Sometimes, life gets overwhelming. So many meetings, fires to put out, crooked places to set straight, sick persons to visit, and don't even get me started on taking care of a spouse and a child. Sometimes, life gets like that—out of hand and uncontrolled. Meeting all the demands before us can be exhausting. When we become overwhelmed, we can easily misstep or even miss what God is saying to us. When our to-do list runs ridiculously long, it is tempting to pull the covers over our heads and just sleep. Yet, that's not an option for us. Why? Because we are called to produce!

We must find ways to deal with and manage the minutiae of everyday life; we can easily get lost in the details and miss the big picture. We have to de-clutter our lives—emotionally, physically, and spiritually. Too much is piling in on us, and something has to change.

Yet, the day begins with us just getting up. When you want to give up or are overwhelmed by the responsibilities you have, you must start the process of moving forward by getting up! I have found that when I get up, God will somehow put moving in my feet!

Lying "there" won't accomplish anything. Stopping now won't bring you any peace. Throwing in the towel will not set a stellar example for the women in ministry who will come behind you.

Too many are dependent on your willingness to stay on the battlefield. Get up!

Some women need to "Get back up" or "Get back in the saddle." No setback should take you out. No failure should derail your passion. The process toward action begins by rising each day, grateful for the fact that you are alive and knowing the daily purpose for our lives are revealed as we move forward. Paraphrasing a saying by Lao-tzu, the journey of a thousand miles begins with a first step. You can't take that step lying down! Get up!

We make the road by walking it, BUT it begins with our getting up and committing to completing the day's assignments. What do you need to finish today? What do you need to start today? What steps must be done today to check off that item on your to-do list that has been there forever? Get up and do something, anything—just get up!

Step Back: Today, clean out that junk drawer. Everybody has one, and we all make promises to de-clutter. The task can be too large so we don't do anything. But just tackle one drawer—throw out what you don't need or don't use. Leave the closets for another day. Do it today!

Perseverance

Day: 6

The Fuel Tank Matters

The Lord is my shepherd, I lack nothing.
He makes me lie down in green pastures,
he leads me beside quiet waters,
he refreshes my soul.
He guides me along the right paths
for his name's sake.
Even though I walk
through the darkest valley,
I will fear no evil,
for you are with me;
your rod and your staff,
they comfort me.

--Psalm 23:1-4

*I*N 1985, during the Daytona 500 auto race, professional racecar driver Donnie Allison was driving a $250,000 car specifically designed for the race. He had practiced. The car was perfectly tuned. Yet, it was on his third lap that the car rolled to a stop on the infield side of the track. Nothing was mechanically wrong with the car. Neither was there anything wrong with the driver.

It was soon discovered, upon closer examination, that, in the hustle and bustle of doing everything that had to be done to prepare the car for the race, somebody forgot to make sure there was enough fuel in the car for it to go the distance. Donnie Allison was out of gas.

The skill of the driver and the potential of the car were completely nullified because somebody forgot to put gas in the car. No matter how much he had practiced, he couldn't move when it mattered because he had no gas. No matter how much he had mastered the course or how much he had invested in the car's design, without the gas needed to go, Allison was stuck on the sidelines.

Perhaps you can't figure out why you find yourself on the sidelines of ministry in this season. Is your gas gone? You aren't sure when it began—that persistent tiredness. You go to bed tired and wake up tired. If we are really honest, it seems the worst on Mondays. You want to "go," but you simply have no "gas" to get to your destination.

Things that were so easy to accomplish before, now take forever to get done. You dread the next meeting; you procrastinate over the report that you have to prepare and deliver. Even getting started on, let alone finishing, that sermon is a huge chore. It's the overwhelming reality of this ever-growing to-do list.

When you can't remember the last time you laughed or enjoyed a meal with a loved one, you are in a state of burn-out and spiritual fatigue. It seems that there is always something—something to do, something that steals your joy, something that keeps you from enjoying life and ministry.

This happens to all of us. I suggest that you are tired in your spirit. It's not about a good night's rest; it is much bigger than that. The joy you had when you first started out just is not there like it used to be.

As ministers and leaders, we burn out! We must be in tune with the feelings and symptoms of burnout. This looming shadow of burnout happens over time. We don't wake up burnt out. It chips away at us, little by little. Until one day we realize that what we thought was held at bay is now sitting squarely in our lap. When we see burnout approaching, we must LISTEN to hear the still, small voice.

What I have found is that most of us won't give ourselves permission to take a time-out. If you don't give yourself permission, you will lose yourself to the shadows that seek to eat you alive and stall your ministry indefinitely.

Over and over again in scripture, it says that Jesus stopped and "went off to a solitary place." Don't you deserve some time with the Good Shepherd? You owe it to yourself and those you lead to pull away and face the reality that you may have overextended yourself in this season of ministry. Perhaps, God is leading you to a rest stop. Give yourself a break. Turn on your hazard lights and pull over before there is a serious problem.

Step Back: The path to renewal is helped by being still. Take a ten-minute break; turn off the phone and iPad or tablet; take a break by going offline—not forever, just ten minutes! Breathe! While that phone is silent, while you ignore Facebook and Twitter, take several deep breaths. Take REAL breaths from the diaphragm. Feel the oxygen moving to every organ. Let God just breathe on you, and you honor the gift of breath. Thank God for the gift of breath. Feel your body relax. Do it now!

Balance

Day: 7

The Secret Garden

Do not be deceived: God cannot be mocked. A man reaps what he sows. Whoever sows to please their flesh, from the flesh will reap destruction; whoever sows to please the Spirit, from the Spirit will reap eternal life. Let us not become weary in doing good, for at the proper time we will reap a harvest if we do not give up. Therefore, as we have opportunity, let us do good to all people, especially to those who belong to the family of believers.

--Galatians 6:7-10

ONE OF MY FAVORITE MOVIES as a child was *The Secret Garden*. It is the story of a girl who loses her parents and goes to live with her uncle. On his property, there is a garden that has been locked up for years. When the little girl finds the garden, it looks a mess. None of her friends believes that she can bring the garden back to life, but the little girl is determined.

She spends her days working in the garden. Pulling up weeds, rinsing off old furniture, restoring pebbled pathways. She knows in her heart that the garden can be made whole again! In due time, her hard work pays off, and she witnesses a small sprout of green. That small sprout of green is all she needs to propel her full speed ahead. Over time, the garden is restored to its full beauty.

Her green came as a result of her hard work. My father raised me to work hard and expect big results. He was right. Too often we can get caught up in who is not working with us. However, the Bible tells us that the workers are few. Yet, a few workers can generate a great harvest. What work, that is seemingly too large, is God calling you to get started on? Nothing will be handed to you. If we do the work, though, God will show up.

I have learned in my tenure as a pastor to not focus on who is not willing to work but to pray fervently for those who will work with me. Pray for your remnant of workers. The numbers may be small, but that small group of workers will assist you in generating a harvest. Pray for their minds. Pray for their strength. Pray for their focus. Pray for their commitment to God. The workers may be few, but God has great plans for a harvest if you won't give up.

We must begin to look for a small sprout of green. It is around us —if we will look closely—God sends these small signs if we will look for them. The full responsibility of your ministry assignment is huge, but start working with those who will follow your lead. The little girl in The Secret Garden had to work by herself until her friends would follow her lead. Working alone didn't stop her because she was not afraid of the work. Don't be afraid of the work that God has set before you.

Labor in the vineyard until God gives you the sign, even if it's small, to keep on keeping on. Once you see it, let it encourage you to run on, and see what the end shall be! Take an inventory of your workspace. The green you long to see is on the way.

Step Back: Are there any plants around you? If so, spend some time nurturing a plant or a flower in your personal space— watering, pruning, turning—so all the sides get some light. If there are no plants, buy one today—it can be a small one. Let it be a reminder that life wants to live—in every space where we spend time.

Day : 8

20/20 Vision

Then the Lord replied: "Write down the revelation
and make it plain on tablets so that a herald may
run with it."

--Habakkuk 2:2

*I*N HIS BOOK, An Anthropologist on Mars, neurologist Oliver Sacks tells about Virgil, a man who had been blind from early childhood. When he was fifty, Virgil underwent surgery and was given the gift of sight. But as he and Dr. Sacks found out, having the physical capacity for sight is not the same as seeing.

Virgil's first experiences with sight were confusing. He was able to make out colors and movements, but arranging them into a coherent picture was more difficult. Over time, he learned to identify various objects, but his habits—his behaviors—were still those of a blind man. He had to learn to live with 20/20 vision.

Dr. Sacks asserts, "One must die as a blind person to be born again as a seeing person. It is the interim, the limbo . . . that is so terrible." To truly see the vision God has and choose to bring it forth into reality, one must see the vision clearly enough to break it into tangible and bite size pieces that create buy-in from our followers.

Almost like Virgil, I have horrible eyesight. You don't even want to know how bad it is. Let's just say that, if they ever changed the "E" at the top of the chart, I would be found out! But it does take me some time to adjust once I put my contacts in or glasses on. With help, I can have nearly 20/20 vision.

The term 20/20 vision expresses "normal" visual acuity; it is a fancy way of measuring how clearly and how sharply one can see. Using this system of measuring vision, 20/20 is the norm—some see better than 20/20 and some see worse than that. Vision that is 20/20 is not necessarily perfect vision, but it is the baseline for good eyesight. However, seeing includes other skills like peripheral awareness or side vision. Peripheral vision keeps us safe. Hand and eye coordination assists us in moving forward and makes everyday life possible. Depth perception helps us to identify what we are looking at. Focusing assists us in seeing clearly. All of this goes into seeing. Every aspect and element work together to provide us with a clear picture that our brains and, if need be, our bodies can understand.

As a child, I remember that pilots were required by Federal law to have 20/20 vision in order to fly a plane. It was believed that pilots who did not have perfect vision could not be trusted with the lives of passengers.

The same goes for us who are in ministry. People don't want to follow someone who can't see clearly. It's not just your ability to see; good leaders have peripheral vision, hand-eye coordination, depth perception, and a host of other skills that assist them in being visionary leaders who people want to follow. People want to be sure that their leader can see well; nobody has the time to follow someone who isn't focused or is dependent on some outside force to help them see (glasses, contacts). Your ability to see in the flesh has no bearing on your ability to see God and follow God's direction.

Too often I find colleagues unfocused. Are the tasks you are working on assisting in making the vision God has given you a reality? Have you clearly communicated the vision God has given you, and have you made it tangible enough for those who follow you to see where they fit or where they can work to help make it come to pass? You cannot do everything, but God will divinely equip you to do the things that make the vision possible. Isn't it time you adjust your eyes by reviewing the vision and ensuring that you are clearly seeing the task before you? Have you talked to those under your leadership and ensured they understand the vision?

Annually, I give my staff a blank sheet of paper and ask them to write out the vision we are working toward. I don't want the vision statement regurgitated to me. I want to hear the reality we are working toward as a group. Hearing their written responses tells me if I have communicated the vision clearly or if I have missed something. If everyone understands the vision except one or two people, then I may need to spend more concentrated time with them. If nearly everyone is missing the mark on the vision, then I need to go back and figure out how to communicate that vision more effectively. If I "see" it, then I ought to be able to communicate it effectively to those who work in the trenches with me.

Aren't you glad that God helps us to see well? Through God's grace and with the help of the Holy Spirit, we can "see" better than 20/20. God wants to make sure the vision is clear, sharp, and written largely enough that even the runner with bad eyesight can see it. Vision is important to God and should be important to us as leaders. Communicating that vision is equally important to seeing what is possible.

I might have horrible vision in the natural, but I have GREAT vision in the spirit. Do you?

Step Back: Do you have a mission statement and vision statement for your life? Consider writing them down and committing them to memory. Let your mission and vision guide your decision-making today. With the opportunities that come your way, ask yourself, "Does this fit within my mission and/or vision?" If the answer is "yes," move forward. If the answer is "no," give yourself permission to decline the invitation. Stay focused.

Day: 9

Wisdom is like the Air

Moses said to the Lord, "May the Lord, the God who gives breath to all living things, appoint someone over this community to go out and come in before them, one who will lead them out and bring them in, so the Lord's people will not be like sheep without a shepherd."

--Numbers 27:15-17

I ONCE OVERHEARD a woman say to another, "You don't have the sense you were born with." Having good sense and having wisdom go hand-in-hand. This is especially true in ministry. We can have all the head knowledge, but if we don't temper that with wisdom, we are doomed to be ineffective.

Too many women in ministry today think they have all the answers. Their pride prevents them from connecting with other women, especially the veteran women in our circles. We dismiss them as old school with nothing relevant to say to this generation of women in ministry.

Here's the thing—any seasoned woman in ministry has been through some things and has gained insight from her experiences. We can learn a thing or two from them if we take the time to listen. Someone once said, "A wise man learns by the experience of others. An ordinary man learns by his own experience. A fool learns by nobody's experience."

In ministry, leadership, and life, wisdom is imperative. Wisdom helps us know what to do, what not to do, where to go, when to stay, when to talk, when to shut up, how to discern the intentions of others, and even what to anticipate down the line. We can let someone else's mistakes and experiences be our learning posts. We need to humble ourselves and be in relationships with those who possess wisdom. We can learn from them.

There's a story about a proud young man who came to Socrates asking for wisdom. He walked up to the muscular philosopher and said, "O great Socrates, I come to you for wisdom."

Socrates recognized the young man's arrogance. He led the young man through the streets, to the sea, and brought him chest deep into the water. Then he asked, "What do you want?"

"Wisdom, O wise Socrates," said the young man with a smile.

Socrates put his strong hands on the man's shoulders and pushed him under the water. For thirty seconds, Socrates held him there and then let him up. "What do you want?" Socrates asked again.

"Wisdom," the young man said, "O great and wise Socrates."

Socrates pushed him under the water again, and held him there for thirty-five seconds. Then forty seconds. Socrates finally let him up. The man was gasping. "What do you want, young man?"

Between heavy and heaving breaths, the young man wheezed, "Wisdom, O wise and wonderful . . ."

Socrates jammed him back under the water again. Forty seconds passed. Then fifty seconds. Bringing him up, Socrates asked a final time, "What do you want?"

"Air!" the young man screeched. "I need air!"

"When you want wisdom as you have just wanted air, then you will have wisdom."

When we are trying to pursue the purpose God has for us, wisdom is our most valuable asset. We ought to want it like air. Wisdom is the steward to greatness. There is a reason Solomon asked God for wisdom. Wisdom, my friend, is priceless.

Step Back: We all know women in ministry who have walked the path we are on. Reach out to such a woman and invite her to coffee. Ask her to share one or two defining moments in her ministry. Listen and learn from her. Don't try to impress her; humble yourself and learn from her! Make the call today!

$\mathcal{D}ay: 10$

I Was Built for This

Then Jesus went with his disciples to a place called Gethsemane, and he said to them, "Sit here while I go over there and pray." He took Peter and the two sons of Zebedee along with him, and he began to be sorrowful and troubled. Then he said to them, "My soul is overwhelmed with sorrow to the point of death. Stay here and keep watch with me."

Going a little farther, he fell with his face to the ground and prayed, "My Father, if it is possible, may this cup be taken from me. Yet not as I will, but as you will."

--Matthew 26:36-39

*L*ET'S BE CLEAR—life is difficult. Those of us in ministry know that this work, while good, can be draining and damaging to our spirits. There are so many demands and responsibilities on us. Yes, it is a privilege to work for God, and, yes, the tasks can threaten to crush us. We have to work to overcome the stress and tensions that come with this level of leadership. Sometimes, friends and colleagues can help us keep things in perspective. And there are times when we have to go for the pity party—where it just feels good to whine, cry, and complain.

I recall one morning I was lying in bed complaining to God about how my current assignment was just too hard ... too difficult ... too painful. As I laid out all the reasons why God should release me from this call, I heard God say back very clearly, "I built you for hard."

It's estimated that there are some 60,000 serious mountain climbers in the U.S. But in the upper echelon of serious climbers is a small, elite group known as "hard men." For them, climbing mountains and scaling sheer rock faces is a way of life. In many cases, climbing is a part of their whole commitment to life. And their ultimate experience is called free soloing: climbing with no equipment and no safety ropes. John Baker is considered by many to be the best of the hard men. He has free soloed some of the most difficult rock faces in the US with no safety rope and no climbing equipment of any kind. His skill has not come easily. It has been acquired through commitment, dedication, and training. His wife says she can't believe his dedication. When John isn't climbing, he can often be found in his California home hanging by his fingertips to strengthen his arms and hands.

As a leader, there is a level of pain, a level of hard, a level of danger, and a level of unique training we must endure in order to make it up the rough side of the mountain. Faith is what has helped us to make it to the top. While you may look all "dolled up" on the outside, all of us have scars underneath from the work of climbing mountains with no equipment and no safety ropes. We are "Hard Women."

If your assignment is hard, good. If your assignment is hard, it should be. The difficulty of your assignment does not mean you can bow out. It simply means you must find a way to endure in a healthy manner. God has a purpose in the midst of your pain. My most painful moments have made me a better leader. My greatest challenges have produced the greatest fruit. My willingness to hang in there has often determined the trajectory of my destiny.

Johnny Fulton was run over by a car at the age of three. He suffered crushed hips, broken ribs, a fractured skull, and compound fractures in his legs. It did not look as if he would live. But he would not give up. As an adult, that broken body was repaired, and he later ran the half-mile in less than two minutes.

Shelly Mann was paralyzed by polio when she was five years old, but she would not give up. She eventually claimed eight different swimming records for the US and won a gold medal at the 1956 Olympics in Melbourne, Australia.

In 1938, Karoly Takacs, a member of Hungary's world-champion pistol shooting team and sergeant in the army, lost his right hand when a grenade he was holding exploded. But Takacs did not give up. He learned to shoot left-handed and won gold medals in the 1948 and 1952 Olympics.

Lou Gehrig was such a clumsy ball player as a child that the boys in his neighborhood would not let him play on their team. His exclusion did not deter his commitment. He did not give up. Eventually, his name was entered into baseball's hall of fame.

Woodrow Wilson could not read until he was ten years old. But he was committed to succeeding. He became the twenty-eighth president of the United States.

Please understand, God has allowed every experience to make you who you are. You were not designed for easy. You were designed for hard. God has confidence in you to not quit but to hang in there and complete your assignment because you were built for this. Today is a day to show God that you can be faithful and trusted with difficulty. Will you pass the test?

Step Back: Today, make a conscious choice to not complain. When a circumstance arises that you could complain about, just thank God for the challenge. Can you make it through the entire day giving God praise for every hard task that comes before you?

Day: 11

Me Time!

Yet the news about him spread all the more, so that crowds of people came to hear him and to be healed of their sicknesses. But Jesus often withdrew to lonely places and prayed.

--Luke 5:15-16

SOMETIMES, we need some "me time"—time away from the hustle and bustle of our days; we need time away from all the hats we wear: wife, mommy, pastor, minister, director, daughter, auntie-- you know those titles that indicate what we should be doing at any given time. Don't you just need a small break to breathe?

A few weeks ago, I was leaving my morning exercise and had a day full of meetings ahead. As I was making my way to my first meeting of the day, our weekly worship meeting with the staff, I heard the Lord say, "Pull over and go in this restaurant and have a cup of coffee and something to eat." I cried out, "But, Lord, if I do that, I will miss the meeting, and you know how crazy this day is." Again, God repeated His sentiments. I pulled my car over. As I sat there, the Lord said to me, "You need thirty minutes of no one calling your name or asking you for anything. You need, for thirty minutes, to be served."

I told the team to meet without me and sat there and enjoyed those thirty minutes. My day went bonkers after I left that restaurant. In fact, it was crazy for the next two weeks. I know that if I had not pulled over for thirty minutes, I would have allowed the spirit of stress to overtake my future days and weeks. It pays to heed God's call to withdraw.

As women in ministry, we are constantly serving. We need to be served every once and a while. We need to take a moment out to let someone bring us a cup of coffee and something to eat. We need a period of time where no one calls our names. We need to heed the call to set aside time when no one wants anything from us.

Don't apologize for a little "me time." As much as you serve others, you deserve it. If Jesus took the time out, why can't you? We can't always take a day or week to renew and refresh. However, you have to monitor your own temperature. Water boils at 212 degrees. If you are at 211 degrees, all is well. Yet, one degree can make all the difference. One degree changes your temperament. One degree can set you over the edge. You must be in tune with your internal temperature and know how to manage it well. There are times when you must stop everything in order to keep yourself from boiling over. We must learn to do this without apology.

Give yourself permission to keep from boiling over. Good leaders understand that mistakes are made when we boil over. We can even lose vulnerable followers when we pile too much on our plate and lose track of our internal temperature. You owe it to yourself and your followers to find a way to manage the stress in a healthy way.

I have a favorite chair in my study. Everybody in the house knows that chair is mine—just for me. More and more these days, with all the demands on my time and energy, I feel that if I can just get to my chair, I'll be all right. Getting to the chair allows me just enough time and space to get through whatever is pressing on me and keeps my internal temperature below the boiling point. I don't need a lot of time in the chair, but I do need to sit there sometimes for just five minutes—to catch my breath, to focus, to refuel. My chair is not a vacation on the beach, but it is a place where I have some "me time."

Step Back: Identify some place or spot in your home that is your "me time" spot. Make sure everyone in your home understands that the spot is just for you and that you are not to be disturbed until you leave that spot.

Balance

Day: 12

If You Can't Do It Right...

Do your best to present yourself to God as one
approved, a worker who does not need to be
ashamed and who correctly handles the word of
truth.

--2 Timothy 2:15

SOME OF US ARE OBSESSED with being perfect. Everything has to be just right. I know a woman who agonizes over details of her sermons. She is so busy editing that she misses the gems that the Holy Spirit has dropped into her spirit—her need to be the perfect preacher keeps the Spirit at bay.

There is a difference between doing our best and doggedly seeking perfection. God deserves our best—best efforts, best thoughts, and best actions. We are not perfect and will never be perfect. That's the Good News. Only Jesus was perfect.

Booker T. Washington said, "Excellence is to do a common thing in an uncommon way." Your best is good enough. However, we need to ensure that what we are offering God, our families, and those who follow our leadership is our best. We have to make time to pray and meditate, time to study and write, time to reflect and ponder. We have to do the work—all of the work—and give it our best.

Howard Thurman said that we ought not to ask what the world needs of us. Instead, we should seek that which makes us come alive. He concludes that the world needs people who have come alive. Will it be perfect? No. Will it bless someone? Yes. Will God be pleased? Definitely!

Too often we do things we really don't want to do or things that do not bring us alive. We do things we don't want to do because we are asked. We do them because it is what is expected of us. We do these things because we believe it will look good on our resumes. This type of behavior must stop. So often, when we take on projects and tasks that we are passionless about in order to please others, we do not offer our best.

When we do our best, God honors our efforts and blesses us in ways we cannot even imagine. Good intentions lead to good efforts, which lead to good action. Can you imagine how we might be even better at what gives us passion if we stopped wasting our time giving half of ourselves to other projects for the sake of people-pleasing?

A lighthouse along a bleak coast was tended by a keeper who was given enough oil for one month and told to keep the light burning every night. One day, a woman asked for oil so that her children could stay warm. Then a farmer came. His son needed oil for a lamp so he could read. Still another needed some for an engine. The keeper saw each as a worthy request and measured out just enough oil to satisfy all. Near the end of the month, the tank in the lighthouse ran dry. That night, the beacon was dark, and three ships crashed on the rocks. More than one hundred lives were lost.

When a government official investigated, the man explained what he had done and why. "You were given one task alone," insisted the official. "It was to keep the light burning. Everything else was secondary. There is no defense."

Keep your focus on offering your best to that which you are called. You can't afford to give half efforts to everything, over giving your best to that which you are called to do. There will be many options for how you will invest the "oil" needed to keep your light shining. Many causes may come your way. Yet, too many lives are dependent on your oil keeping the lights on to ensure the safety of all rather than risking half efforts to help a few.

Step Back: Everyone needs a "theme" song—a piece of music that inspires and motivates you no matter what else is happening in your life. Choose a theme song, and listen to it at least once each day—put it on your computer, phone, iPad, iPod, or tablet. Let the music move you through your day and keep you focused on offering your best to that which you are called.

Excellence

Day: 13

Discerning the Time

[Mordecai] he sent back this answer: "Do not think that because you are in the king's house you alone of all the Jews will escape. For if you remain silent at this time, relief and deliverance for the Jews will arise from another place, but you and your father's family will perish. And who knows but that you have come to your royal position for such a time as this?"

--Esther 4:13-14

HERE IS AN OLD-SCHOOL SONG made popular by blues artist B.B. King. The song is entitled "Never Make a Move Too Soon." This statement can mean different things to different people -- and we won't go there!

Here's the thing: the song is about timing. And in life and ministry, timing is everything. We can make decisions in haste rather than take the time to investigate more fully. We can make choices too quickly instead of letting the information marinate. We can jump to conclusions rather than hearing all sides of an issue. When we trust God and God's timing, we can be assured that the right decision, choice, and conclusion will be reached.

It is a simple matter of fact—if we pick fruit before it is ripe, it will be hard, inferior, and tasteless. If we pick fruit too late, it will be mushy, over-ripe, rotten, and tasteless. The key is knowing when the time is right to pluck the fruit from the vine.

An inventor may come out with a product that grabs the market while another equally talented inventor can produce a product that is better than the other one, yet fail. Why? It is all in the timing. A business can open prematurely and result in bankruptcy while another business can flourish all because of timing. An author can write a book that makes the bestseller list while another book, which is better written, can collect dust on the shelves because it came out too early or too late. Timing can make or break a good idea.

As wise Solomon wrote, "He has made everything beautiful in its time" (Ecclesiastes 3:11). What made David's kingdom the greatest in Israel's history was that David's military leaders "understood the times and knew what Israel should do" (1 Chronicles 12:32). Even King Xerxes understood this. Though deficient in moral character, King Xerxes knew to surround himself "with the wise men who understood the times" (Esther 1:13). This kept him in power for life.

When it comes to making a decision about ministry, we should slow down and wait for God to speak, for the Holy Spirit to guide, and for Jesus to lead all at the right time. One of the most valuable lessons I have learned is that, despite what others may lead me to believe, "time is on my side." It's just that we rarely figure out how much time we have to make the right decisions. We let others rush us before God is ready to guide us, or we allow others to hold us back in fear. We make dangerous errors this way.

We rush in because we think we know God's answer, based on our own logic and not God's directions. When we do, disaster is sure to follow. However, if we wait on the Lord, marvelous things can happen. Discerning the time is a sign of maturity in the faith and in our calling. God will make all things plain—if we tune into

God's frequency and wait for God's nudging. I can guarantee you that waiting on God's timing is always the right thing to do.

Step Back: Is there something in your ministry that you have been putting off? Is the time right for that action now? If so, make a commitment to do it. If not, ask God for the patience to wait for the right time.

Day: 14

Relationship Management

The words of the reckless pierce like swords, but the tongue of the wise brings healing.

--Proverbs 12:18

A S CLERGY, we have all been there. We see the phone ring, and when the caller ID displays the name, we know instantaneously that the person on the other end wants something. If the truth be told, this person only calls when they need something. They never check on us. They never take us out to lunch to say thanks for all the help we offered last time. We see their name, and we know that they will ask us to pull a rabbit out of a hat. We don't mind helping out and doing what we can, but is the basis of our relationship only what I can do for you?

While you know what it is like to feel this way about the caller on the other end, I wonder if there is someone in your life who sees your name and thinks the same of you. You only call when you need something. You only call when times are tough. You never ask if you can be a blessing to that person in any way. With your name, comes a resonance with "a want."

When we hit the roadblocks of life, we often call upon those we know possess wisdom or connections to help get us out of our tough spots. We do a horrible job of relationship management if we only call on the wise when we need something. Is what we "get" from them all that matters in this relationship? I don't think

Christ "uses" people. Our relationship with Christ is a give and take.

The last time someone helped you out, did you drop them a handwritten note of thanks? Did you take them to lunch as a sign of appreciation? Did you tell them how the situation panned out and thank them for their assistance? Did you send them flowers? What kind gesture did you extend to them as a sign of your genuine and sincere gratitude?

Relationship management, when everything is well, plays a significant role in gaining wisdom and insight in times of trouble. Today you need to write a few notes of thanks. It might be a good idea to simply check on the person who helps you out from time to time.

It doesn't just have to be those whom you call upon when you need a favor. Take time out to check on those who help you do ministry effectively week in and week out. Ask them how things are going and if there is any way you can be a blessing to them in this season. Managing all of these relationships with more intentionality will be a blessing to you and help you to navigate in the future.

Let's also not forget our mentors. Over and over they impart wisdom in our lives. We need to thank them for being our sounding board or even teaching us how to do ministry more effectively. These folks have helped shape us into effective ministers of the gospel. It will be good for them to see your name on their caller ID and not want a thing but to check on them.

Isn't it time you bless the team that has helped you achieve the measure of success you have seen thus far? Say a prayer for each team member individually. Thank God for the gift of putting each person in your life.

Step Back: Call up someone who has blessed you in times of trouble, and tell them thank you. If finances permit, select a meaningful gift for them, and show them what a blessing they have been to your life. Now is the time to pour back into those who have poured into you.

$\mathcal{D}ay: 15$

It Doesn't Just Happen

Brothers and sisters, I do not consider myself yet to have taken hold of it. But one thing I do: Forgetting what is behind and straining toward what is ahead, I press on toward the goal to win the prize for which God has called me heavenward in Christ Jesus.

--Philippians 3:13-14

"SEE, WHAT HAD HAPPENED WAS..." How many times have you heard that? How many times have you said that? These words are usually the beginning of a long, drawn-out story that has very little to do with the situation at hand. These words lead us to think that things just happen—without cause and without purpose.

When it comes to ministry and leadership—things rarely just happen. I believe we can learn something from every single situation that happens to us and around us—sometimes, we have to dig deep, and sometimes, we just have to wait for the lesson to be revealed.

It is true that, while we are waiting, we can become discouraged and disappointed. There is nothing worse than operating in a season where nothing seems to be coming together as planned. Our phone calls are not being returned. Emails are bouncing back. Individuals who committed to keeping deadlines, with good intentions, can't even remember making the promise in the first place. We are often running late. Sermons are unfinished. Letters still haven't been written to the congregation. It seems to be like a domino effect.

This is where your faith comes in. Faith is not blindly believing in something or someone. Faith is the wide-eyed stand we take when we trust that God is up to something in our lives and in our ministries. More than belief, faith is our posture in times of trouble.

Faith is the assurance that, in the midst of what seems desperate, things will be fine in the end. Faith is that "something" on the inside that keeps us standing when we don't want to or can't seem to stand. Faith is that "something" that pushes us on when we don't have any strength on our own. Faith is that "something" that keeps us from giving in, giving up, and giving out.

Where is your faith in this season? Faith, in the beginning of a project or a vision, is often easy to maintain. Yet, it is our faith in the "thick of it" that makes the difference in our ability to finish the task ahead of us. This is the time when big girl faith is required. Not when everything is smooth sailing, but when you can't tell how God is going to work all of this together. Yet, God does.

A few months ago, I had a sore throat. I went to the store and purchased the Halls brand of throat lozenges. As I unwrapped the paper surrounding the lozenge, I noticed that it said, "March Forward." It was the reminder that the call of God is to move forward. You do know that the slogan for Halls is "There's a pep talk in every drop."

With faith, there ought to be a pep talk in every drop. So today is a great day to muster up your faith and keep going. Today is the day to recite scripture, to remind yourself of the many ways God has brought you through. Today is a day to put all that faith in action. If you need to, regroup, by all means. However, don't just choose to "see what happens." Choose intentionally to follow the call of God. Choose to be all God has called you to be. I want to suggest that you decide that, even though you cannot control others, you can control yourself. Today, faith is not choosing what is obvious or convenient. Faith, my sister, is doing just what God said. Faith is changing your posture and believing that what God has for your life shall come to pass. Today, your situation turns around because God has not given up on you, and you have not given up on God. Commit to moving forward by faith!

Step Back: Go online and find an affirmation that speaks directly to you. Make it your screensaver, and write it down so you can see it several times a day.

Perseverance

Day: 16

Pace Yourself

There is a time for everything,
and a season for every activity under the heavens:
a time to be born and a time to die,
a time to plant and a time to uproot,
a time to kill and a time to heal,
a time to tear down and a time to build,
a time to weep and a time to laugh,
a time to mourn and a time to dance,
a time to scatter stones and a time to gather
them,
a time to embrace and a time to refrain from
embracing,
a time to search and a time to give up,
a time to keep and a time to throw away,
a time to tear and a time to mend,
a time to be silent and a time to speak,
a time to love and a time to hate,
a time for war and a time for peace.

--Ecclesiastes 3:1-8

T IS FASCINATING HOW old things can be recycled. This even happens with language. Take the word "tether," for instance. Yes, tether is an old school word. It means a rope or chain with which an animal is tied to restrict its movement. In everyday terms, being tethered means being tied down to something that keeps us from going where we want to go or doing what we want to do. Being tethered is a negative and oppressive thing.

Technology has taken that word and given it a new meaning; it means using a smartphone in order to connect a computer or other device to the Internet. Tethering is a good thing, allowing access to power that had not been there before. That power—the power of technology—has us tethered in a new way. We are tethered to our electronic devices. Almost everyone is connected somehow—through smartphones, iPhones, iPads, tablets—we hardly look at anyone anymore because our heads are glued to those little screens.

Walk down any street and see how many people have phones to their ears or have their fingers tapping out text and email messages. Even the esteemed New Yorker magazine sported a cover of a family of four, dressed in vacation clothes on a beach—each with a phone in hand and paying no attention to one another.

Within the context of ministry, people use their electronic devices to make their emergency, your emergency. A call, email, or text comes in, and we spring into action with no sense of what God is calling us to do in this very present moment. When is the last time you assessed the season? Are you always rescuing? Always answering? Always replying? Is your electronic device setting the tone and pace of your day?

This lifestyle is not sustainable. We have to find balance—time for self, time for others, and certainly, time for God. We are so used to multitasking that we are losing the art of conversation and being with others. It's time to unplug!

If the truth be told, it's hard to hear God with our device notifications, sounds, tones, and alerts. We can't even sit through thirty minutes of prayer without our phones going off. If we allow it, this technology will swallow us up and prevent us from hearing God clearly.

When is the last time you fasted from electronic devices? When is the last time you determined that social media or technology would not set the tone of your day? When was the last time you ignored the mass messages coming through?

As women in ministry, we already have so many calling our names and demanding our attention, we open up another platform for this with our electronic devices. Can you hear God calling your name? Perhaps God is unwilling to yell over the noise of your life to be heard. Maybe God wants to know if you can hear Him, his gentle whisper, which is absent of technology. Isn't it time to find balance and untie the "tether" you have created with your device?

By strengthening the "tether" of your relationship with God, you will find access to new power and a fresh wind. God wants to breathe on you and longs to do that device-free. Today, have a love affair with Him and tie yourself to his well, which never runs dry.

Step Back: We don't always have time to renew and refresh. We do have time to reconnect with nature. Take a five-minute walk with no electronic devices. If you can, manage a longer walk. Pay attention to the sounds you hear; identify all the different colors of vegetation you see; notice what's moving as you stroll. Breathe deeply as you walk, and see how you feel.

Balance

Day: 17

Be Yourself

"You are the light of the world. A town built on a hill cannot be hidden. Neither do people light a lamp and put it under a bowl. Instead they put it on its stand, and it gives light to everyone in the house. In the same way, let your light shine before others, that they may see your good deeds and glorify your Father in heaven."

--Matthew 5:14-16

A WISE PERSON ONCE SAID that imitation is the highest form of flattery, or something like that. Today, imitation may be the basis for a lawsuit.

Women in ministry sometimes compete with other women in ministry. They put other women down in order to make themselves feel better, worthy, enough. God does not honor our actions when we gossip about, wish ill for, or belittle other women. We are all gifted; no one has the market on giftedness. In other words, we are not in competition with one another. God calls us to be fully who we are, with all of our gifts and flaws. Our calling is to present our best to God—my best, not anyone else's.

Ministry and leadership excellence is only about my best. God knew what he was doing in calling you, me, and others into the ministry. We don't need to feel jealous, envious, or inadequate. We don't have to define our success in ministry by the success of another sister. We have all we need to be fitting disciples for Jesus and God.

The story is told of a little candle that stood in a room filled with other candles. Most of the other candles seemed larger and more beautiful than she was. Some were ornate, and some were rather simple, like her. Some were brown, some were blue, some were pink, some were green, and some were white. She had no idea why she was there, and the other candles made her feel rather small and insignificant.

When the sun went down and the room began to get dark, the candle noticed a large man walking toward her with a ball of fire on a stick. She suddenly realized that the man was going to set her ablaze.

To her surprise, the room filled with light. She wondered where it came from since the man had extinguished his fire stick. To her delight, she realized that the light came from her.

Then the man struck another fire stick and, one by one, lit the other candles in the room. Each one gave out the same light that she did until the room was filled with light. Without her light, the room would not be able to be as bright. She needed the other candles to shine, and they needed her.

This is what we need as women in ministry. We need our light to shine in its own unique ways. Comparing ourselves to others is a slippery slope to deceit and inauthenticity. God called you to be you, not to be a cheap imitation of someone else. When will you gain the confidence to know what God wants of you, flaws and all? What is powerful in ministry and is the hallmark of a true leader is authenticity, one who chooses to genuinely let her light shine as bright as Christ will allow. We must learn to embrace who we are and trust God to use our uniqueness. We will never measure up to others—we are enough, just as we are. Our duty is to give our best to God. That, my sister, is Good News.

Step Back: Today, take a good look at yourself in the mirror. What do you do well? What gifts do you bring to ministry? What are your strengths? After you've had a good talk with yourself, say a prayer for confidence in who God has created you to be. Let your inner light shine today!

Excellence

Day: 18

Bigger Than Me!

"Whoever serves me must follow me; and where I am, my servant also will be. My Father will honor the one who serves me."

--John 12:26

I LOVE THE TELEVISION SHOW Undercover Boss. It is a reality-based program where corporate executives disguise themselves as "regular" workers and spend time on the front lines of their companies to assess how things are going. They seek to make sure every person in the company understands the mission of the corporation.

The undercover bosses have fielded customer service phone calls, taken out trash, mopped floors, and staffed drive-thru windows at fast food restaurants. No job is too small for these top executives. They are always humbled by their hands-on experiences and go on to make changes to benefit their workers.

There is no job too big or too small for me to do in the church where I serve. I've preached to the crowds and to the few. I've cleaned the toilets and unstopped sinks. My call is to be a servant–leader. So I never think I am better than anyone else—we are all servants of Jesus with different gifts.

To be a real visionary leader, you need to be able to see all the parts and pieces. When we humble ourselves, we are reminded that we take for granted so many who work to make the vision a reality and are often overlooked. You build a visionary team when you remember that everyone helps to make it happen and no job is beneath you.

Periodically, we need to revisit our calling to make sure we understand the mission and movement of God. I am always thinking about what God is calling me to do—and when I hear God's voice, I do whatever it is. No matter how big or how small, obedience and humility is my aim. God honors sincere intentions and actions. God honors Jesus's servant ministry and leadership. God will honor ours as well.

Step Back: Take some time today to write down the circumstances surrounding your call to ministry and leadership. Think about where you were and what you were doing when you heard God's call. If you have already written this event down, re-read and reflect on it. Determine if you are living your call more fully now.

$\mathcal{D}ay$: 19

Write the Vision

And afterward,
I will pour out my Spirit on all people.
Your sons and daughters will prophesy,
your old men will dream dreams,
your young men will see visions.
Even on my servants, both men and women,
I will pour out my Spirit in those days.

--Joel 2:28-29

*G*REAT LEADERS HAVE VISION. Great leaders see things that ordinary people do not. These people inspire others to follow. Have you thought about what Jesus said to the disciples? While they were going about their everyday work and tasks, Jesus showed up and said, "Follow me!" What was it about Jesus's tone, demeanor, or look that made women and men stop their livelihoods, give up their homes, abandon their relationships, and take off on a journey with him? Notice that Jesus did not lay out before them a ten-point plan; he didn't present a dissertation on how to live an abundant life through logical investments; he didn't have an app for bringing people to God.

Jesus had a vision and shared his vision with them. He demonstrated and embodied his vision. Writing instructors constantly tell their students to "show, don't tell." By this, they seek to encourage students to draw pictures so others can see and visualize what it is they want to convey.

People follow those who can articulate what they see and what they believe. Think about it. Martin L. King, Jr.'s power was in the authenticity of his presentations, sermons, and speeches. He spoke from his heart, and his passion came from the vision God had given him. There were others who spoke on the issues plaguing black people in the 1950s and 1960s. What set Dr. King apart from the others was the passion of his conviction—people believed that he believed what he was saying. There was so much conviction and passion in what he said that others were convinced he was right. They wanted to be a part of the movement.

Great leadership happens when we let God set the agenda. We must be willing to let God be the author and finisher of all that we do. When we are anointed by the Holy Spirit, we see what others cannot. The vision is what inspires us and keeps us encouraged on the journey.

Nelson Mandela once said that everything is impossible until it is done. It is God who gives the impossible dream, the improbable vision, and the unlikely mission.

God gave Dr. King a dream, and it was up to others to develop a plan around that dream. Great leaders surround themselves with others who see something they also see—it is said that great minds think alike.

The same can be said of our leadership and ministry. When we connect with others who see what we see, we can be assured of success. This does not mean we should surround ourselves with people who never disagree with us; there is no room for "yes" folks when a vision is at stake. What we want to do is to surround ourselves with smart and gifted people who help us sharpen the vision and help us bring the vision to fulfillment.

We often poke fun at Jesus's disciples. Too often, they seemed dim-witted and a step behind Jesus in understanding the vision and mission. Yet their questions and misunderstandings were opportunities for Jesus to clarify the vision, to make the mission plain, and to keep them focused on the important aspects of the work. God calls us to continue dreaming, prophesying, and envisioning. All we have to do is make space for the Holy Spirit to work.

And God calls those of us in leadership to make space for everyone to dream; from dreaming, we get great ideas, strategies, and blueprints for constructing plans according to God's design. The important thing is to be clear about what we believe—to state clearly and plainly what we believe—and others will connect with us and lend their hands and hearts to the mission.

Step Back: Look at how much time you have in this season of ministry from now until the end of the year. Where do you envision your ministry being by the end of the year? Write the vision and the intentional steps you will take to make the vision a reality. Evaluate your growth every six to twelve weeks. Are you on track? Has the vision evolved?

$\mathcal{D}$ay: 20

Doubt

"Lord, if it's you," Peter replied, "tell me to come to you on the water."
"Come," he said.
Then Peter got down out of the boat, walked on the water and came toward Jesus. But when he saw the wind, he was afraid and, beginning to sink, cried out, "Lord, save me!"
Immediately Jesus reached out his hand and caught him. "You of little faith," he said, "why did you doubt?"
And when they climbed into the boat, the wind died down. Then those who were in the boat worshiped him, saying, "Truly you are the Son of God."

--Matthew 14:28-33

E BEGIN OUR MINISTRIES with high hopes and expectations. We have climbed up the rough sides of mountains to achieve educational goals. We have trudged through all the hoops that are required for us to move into positions of leadership. When we have done the work, we expect results. When we crash into glass ceilings, we are disappointed. When we run head-on into walls that impede our progress, we are frustrated. When the acclaim and fame are elusive, we are disillusioned. Our insecurities and doubts take center stage.

When we face stumbling blocks and delays of all sorts, we become discouraged. Ministry has a rhythm—it ebbs and flows. There are mountaintop and valley experiences. There are sunshine days and cloudy ones. When we are in the valley, we begin to question everything—our calling, our purpose, and our vision. It is common for us to have moments of uncertainty and doubt.

It is important to remember that valley experiences teach us things about ourselves and about God. We need to ask ourselves those hard questions: Why am I in this valley? Did I do something or fail to do something for a different outcome? What do I need to work on to make myself better fit for leadership? How is God strengthening me to climb mountains? Who can help me overcome my doubts?

Being in the valley is uncomfortable. We would rather be hitting our stride with confidence and poise. We want to be in control and chart our destinies. Too often, we want to rush through the valley in order to get back to the top of the mountain. Yet, when we try to rush through the valley, we miss the lesson and the blessing. God tries to tell us something in that valley.

When I completed seminary, I thought I would receive a call immediately. I had done all the work. I had prepared myself. My credentials were in order. I was ready. Despite all my efforts, however, I waited and waited. In the beginning of my search for a ministry position, I did not receive the requests for interviews. I did not receive the call I longed for and for which I had prepared. It was a valley time for me. I had some long and painful talks with God. I started to think I had misheard God's call. I didn't know what to do. To date, that was one of my darkest seasons in ministry. I had done all I could. My only option was to pray and wait. I prayed and cried and yelled at God. It seemed that I had put everything on the line for God, but God was not responding to my efforts. I certainly was not receiving the rewards I thought I deserved. I was in a valley—a deep valley. On certain days, I reminded myself over and over, "While this is a really bad chapter of my life, it is not the last chapter of my life."

I constantly asked God what lesson I was to learn while in the valley. I waited to hear God's voice, waited for some hint or clue that God, indeed, had called me for a reason and for a purpose. My faith deepened as I sought the presence and power of God to move in my life and to anoint my ministry.

I learned that God's time was not my time. I learned what real peace in God looks like. I learned the value of earnest prayer. I learned that patience is a virtue that is developed in valley times. I learned that God showed up in the little things in my day and week—the money that appeared right on time, the invitation to share a meal with a friend willing to listen to me, the sunshine after a snowstorm, the rush of emotion while listening to a good sermon, the peace that comes after laying my burdens before God. In these and other things, I learned that God had not forsaken or forgotten about me. I learned to wait upon the Lord, and God always showed up. Each and every time!

We all have doubts from time to time. Keep praying and pressing your way into God's presence. God will be there.

Step Back: When you are feeling especially discouraged and fatigued, anoint yourself with oil as a reminder that God's got your back. Better yet, gather a group of ministry colleagues to pray and anoint one another.

Perseverance

Day: 21

Intentionality

*"I am the true vine, and my Father is the gardener.
He cuts off every branch in me that bears no fruit,
while every branch that does bear fruit he prunes
so that it will be even more fruitful. You are already
clean because of the word I have spoken to you.
Remain in me, as I also remain in you. No branch
can bear fruit by itself; it must remain in the vine.
Neither can you bear fruit unless you remain in me.
"I am the vine; you are the branches. If you remain
in me and I in you, you will bear much fruit; apart
from me you can do nothing."*

--John 15:1-5

EFFECTIVE LEADERSHIP HAPPENS in a context where there is focus, purpose, and action. A centerpiece of good leadership is healthy relationships. We know that good relationships don't just happen. Intentionality is the glue that holds relationships together.

Think about one of your most meaningful relationships. What makes that relationship work? How does that relationship make you a better person? I imagine that your list includes time, love, commitment, communication, patience, forgiveness, and intentionality. In order for any relationship to grow and thrive, we need to attend to it, or the relationship will wither and die. Even worse, it may become superficial.

The same holds true for leadership and ministry. At the center of our work should be the Triune God—our reason for being. All the tasks we do serve the purpose of creating relationships of trust and collaboration—we work together to get things done. In order for this to happen, we must be intentional about our interactions with others.

When is the last time you checked on the folks who work in the trenches with you? I'm not talking about a superficial, "Hey, how are you doing?" I mean, when is the last time you really checked in with those who serve alongside you?

So often, we notice when people aren't on their post. We call them up to ask why they aren't producing, but we don't pause to see how life is treating them. Really treating them. Isn't it time we tap into those who serve with us? You can "think" you know the context of their lives, but until you really sit down and listen, you would be surprised.

This does not mean we are everywhere, doing everything. It doesn't mean we pull out the church's phone directory and just start dialing. Intentionality means we prioritize those who have made us and our call a priority.

No one is saying you have to check in with everyone today. We must keep boundaries. We must choose quality over quantity. We can totally wear ourselves out if we don't take the time to determine what is important, who we can create authentic time with today, and what can wait until another day or time.

Jesus did not heal all the sick people of his day. He did not teach on every text of scripture. He did not address every issue and concern of the people during his time. His ministry was focused and intentional. He invested in the twelve who were consistently with him. He performed enough miracles and taught enough scripture for the ordinary person to understand that God's Kingdom was in their midst if they would take the time to look and listen.

Our ministries must be focused and intentional. We must invest in those who have sacrificed for the vision God has given us to become a reality. We pay attention to the big picture and the details, but we don't get lost in the midst of it all. We work with purpose and on purpose. We must be clear; very little we do is done in isolation. Intentionality is active, not passive; it is directed, not haphazard.

Step Back: Make a list of twelve people who have worked closely with you in this season of ministry. Reach out to one to two people a day by checking in with them. Commit to calling all twelve over the next few days. Start today.

Balance

Day: 22

Setting a Standard

Therefore, my dear brothers and sisters, stand firm.
Let nothing move you. Always give yourselves fully
to the work of the Lord, because you know that
your labor in the Lord is not in vain.

--1 Corinthians 15:58

THERE IS A LEADERSHIP STORY circulating about a rich man who wanted to build his dream home. He hired a contractor and gave him an unlimited budget. The man described his lifestyle and his values. The man wanted a home he could be proud of and that would provide a comfortable living space for his family. The man was about to go away on a long trip and placed his trust in the contractor. With money being no object, the man was confident that the contractor would construct a sturdy and luxurious abode.

The contractor decided to cut corners and pocket the money for himself. Because his morals were low, so were the morals of all the sub-contractors he hired. They cut even more corners. Since the contractor had low expectations, the construction workers felt no need to preserve their relationship.

He thought that, because the owner was not there to supervise him, he could do whatever he wanted. With the money, the contractor could move to a remote island and would never have to account for the shoddy work of the house.

When the owner returned from his trip, he saw the house and was impressed. It looked good on the outside, but when he inspected the interior, he noticed the shoddy work. He understood what the contractor had done and came up with a way to hold the man accountable.

The owner told the contractor that the house was much too beautiful and luxurious for his own family. He gave the house to the contractor in lieu of the final payment. The owner explained that the house was worth more than he could ever pay the contractor. The stunned contractor was left with a sub-par house because he placed money above good workmanship.

Because the contractor schemed and cheated, he was left with a pretty house that had no substance. Any powerful storm would come along and destroy the house he built. This is a leadership lesson—give your best effort because you never know how you will be held accountable for your assignments.

People are watching us. They watch to see how we handle ourselves in various situations. Some watch for us to stumble and fall. Some watch to cheer us on. Some watch so they can follow our example. In all that we do, we must do our best, every single time.

Effective leadership requires insight, wisdom, common sense, and our very best work effort. It is up to us to set the tone for excellence in our workplaces and our homes. Staff and volunteers will only rise to your level of expectation. If your work ethic is low, theirs will be too. You are the leader, and they will follow your lead.

You know, that great hymn of the church "Only What You Do for Christ Will Last" has the right theology. When we cut corners, when we give less than our best, when we do what is easiest, when we think no one will notice, we are on a slippery slope downward.

Because God has given the very best of everything, we give back our best. This does not mean we must be perfect; it means that we do the best that our abilities and gifts will bear. When we do our best, we inspire others to do the same.

We must set the bar high because we work for God. How can we do anything less than our best when God has given us so much? Let us strive to offer our best effort and intention to the building of God's Realm.

Step Back: Do something today that is outside of your comfort zone. Write your mission, vision statement, or a verse from your theme song with your non-dominant hand (if you are right-handed, write with your left; if left-handed, write with your right); take a different route to work or home; shake up your routine for one day, but give it your best no matter what. Explore your feelings about the change.

Day: 23

A Second Look

When Jesus spoke again to the people, he said, "I am the light of the world. Whoever follows me will never walk in darkness, but will have the light of life."

--John 8:12

I LOVE DIAMONDS. Have you ever seen a jeweler assess a diamond? A standard piece of equipment is the jeweler's loupe. This device is a lens that magnifies the image of the diamond so all the details are apparent. The jeweler can see aspects not noticeable to the naked eye. Through the loupe, the jeweler is able to detect internal flaws (inclusions) as well as any external flaws (blemishes). The jeweler will turn the diamond over and over in order to assess its worth. Diamonds are ranked according to carat, color, cut, and clarity. The point is to help the buyer get the best diamond for her budget. Buyers want diamonds that sparkle and shine with as few flaws as possible.

Imagine that your vision is a diamond. Periodically, we need to re-assess the vision God has given us. We need to review and see where we are in our work to bring the vision to fruition. It is imperative that we take a step back from time to time to make sure we are staying the course.

In other words, we need to take a second look at our vision. The call is solid and things change as we move our vision forward. Circumstances can change; personnel can change; resources can change; we can change. All of these and more have to be factored in as our vision unfolds.

Sometimes, we forge ahead with our vision and become frustrated when things start to get off track. We have tunnel vision and refuse to see the signs that we need to check things out again. Evaluation, or taking a second look, helps us determine if we need to make adjustments. When we engage in honest evaluation, we are not blindsided by changes because we've taken the time to do some assessment of where we are in light of where we want to go.

Failure to step back may prevent us from stepping up and stepping forward. Only honest assessment can ensure that we are staying the course. One of the joys of reading the Bible is that, every time we do, we find something we hadn't seen before. There are surprises when we go over old territory. The stories are so familiar that we think we know all there is about the text. Yet, each time, something jumps out at us that has been there all the time but we failed to see it.

I once heard about a new pastor who had a vision for her ministry, and she knew how to implement her vision. During the Christmas season, a Christmas tree appeared in the pulpit. The pastor didn't know who had placed the tree there, but she knew it was the wrong place for it. She had the tree moved to the narthex, but the next Sunday, the tree was back in the pulpit. Again, she had it moved. The next Sunday, the tree mysteriously reappeared in the pulpit. She had the tree removed from the church—decorations, lights, and all. The church council called a special meeting with the pastor. Before the members could say anything, the pastor gave a long speech about the theological reasons for not having a tree in the pulpit. When she had finished her tirade, the council members quietly told her the story about the tree—a member who loved Christmas had provided a tree each year for the church for over twenty years. The member had helped decorate the tree just days before she died. The tree was placed in the pulpit as a memorial to the long-standing member in lieu of the regular altar flowers.

The pastor was so rigid in her leadership style that she never asked anyone in the church about the tree. Because she didn't know the story, she couldn't be intentional and methodical about how to address the issue. This faux pas cost the pastor dearly. She never regained the trust of the members, and they did not get on board with her vision. Had she been able to take a step back, she might have been able to realize the vision she had for the church. Had she stepped back, she may have heard the Spirit whispering, "Get the history." Had she stepped back, there may have been a compromise that moved the vision forward without compromising her theological stance.

It will pay off in the long-run if you take the time to give your vision and leadership style a second look.

Step Back: Revisit your Spiritual Gifts Assessment Inventory from day 2. What would you add now to that list? What concrete things have you done to enhance and develop those gifts?

$\mathcal{D}ay: 24$

Buy-In

*So we rebuilt the wall till all of it reached half its
height, for the people worked with all their heart.*

--Nehemiah 4:6

THE GREAT THING ABOUT NEHEMIAH was that he
did everything from a spiritual perspective. His tender
heart longed to help his people back in Jerusalem.
After a period of fasting and prayer, Nehemiah was given a clear
vision—go back to Jerusalem and help rebuild the city walls.
Cities were built upon hills, and a wall was needed for protection
against invading enemies. Nehemiah knew he could not restore
the entire city, but a defensive wall was the first step in rebuilding
the city. The vision was clear. All he needed was a group of
resourceful people to see the vision and help him.

He was earnest and sincere when he shared the vision. The King of
Persia was so moved that he granted Nehemiah permission to go
to Jerusalem and provided a letter granting safe passage and
material resources (lumber, nails, hammers, mortar, etc.) to get the
job done.

When Nehemiah arrived in Jerusalem, he surveyed the job and
developed his strategy. Only after a thorough investigation and
evaluation did he share his vision with the people. He was so clear
that the people could see what he saw—Jerusalem's walls rebuilt
and the people ready to be restored. They supported him. Every
family pitched in and worked to their capacity. The people seemed

to have been given a temporary set of gifts that they perhaps had not identified prior to his coming. Yet, they were committed to seeing the wall come to fruition.

They had bought into the vision. Of course, there were some obstacles and stumbling blocks. Every good work encounters these. By keeping his eye on the prize, Nehemiah was able to keep the people motivated to complete the work. The people were all in. Even when danger threatened the work, the people remained committed.

The same can happen with our leadership and ministry if we are clear about the vision and if we share it with passion and conviction. How you communicate vision matters. When the vision catches hold, folks will be on board. When the larger vision is broken down into bite-size or tangible pieces, those who hear the vision can find the place where their gifts fit. Followers of the vision will go above and beyond to make the vision a reality. Once they find where they fit, followers will be excited about how the vision unfolds, and they will be proud to be a part of the team.

Who is on your leadership and ministry team? Who understands your vision so clearly they can share it better than you can? What are you doing to keep your team motivated and energized? How have you broken the vision down into bite-size steps? Is there a methodology for bringing the vision forth? A timeline? What are you doing to keep yourself motivated? How do you keep your eye on the prize in the midst of all the things you have to do and be?

The time to figure this out is now. It is the only way to create buy-in. Over and over in the Bible it is clear that God calls us to work with others. Bringing forth this vision God has given you is no different. Now is the time to assemble those who trust the vision God has given you, even when it doesn't make sense.

Step Back: Examine your mission and Values Statements from day 8. Sum up your statements in a slogan that will fit on a T-shirt. Write your slogan down and put it where you can see it on a regular basis. Share it with others in your leadership or ministry setting.

$\mathcal{D}ay$: 25

Hanging In

"No one will be able to stand against you all the days of your life. As I was with Moses, so I will be with you; I will never leave you nor forsake you. Be strong and courageous, because you will lead these people to inherit the land I swore to their ancestors to give them.

"Be strong and very courageous. Be careful to obey all the law my servant Moses gave you; do not turn from it to the right or to the left, that you may be successful wherever you go. Keep this Book of the Law always on your lips; meditate on it day and night, so that you may be careful to do everything written in it. Then you will be prosperous and successful. Have I not commanded you? Be strong and courageous. Do not be afraid; do not be discouraged, for the Lord your God will be with you wherever you go."

--Joshua 1:5-9

OUR TIMES CALL FOR COURAGEOUS LEADERSHIP. These times require leaders who are bold and vocal. Yes, ministry is hard. It's even harder when we succumb to the "walk on water" syndrome. You know—when we think we can do all things for all people. We are so eager to please everyone that we wear ourselves out in the effort. Then, we get angry when folks don't bow down to us or lift us up with their accolades.

It would have been easy for Joshua to refuse the mantle of leadership from Moses. However, Joshua's leadership apprenticeship began when he was very young. He watched Moses lead the people; he watched Moses make adjustments in his leadership style and his strategy after his consultation with his father-in-law, Jethro. He watched Moses interact with and share leadership with Aaron and Miriam. When it was time for Joshua to assume leadership responsibilities, he led with boldness because he had seen Moses in action.

When others were fearful because there were giants in the Promised Land and his own people looked like grasshoppers, Joshua declared that they could take the land. He was bold, courageous, and fearless because he understood the vision.

We are called to bold leadership and ministry. We are called to be faithful to the task God gives us. When our will is aligned with God's will for us, we have strength for the journey. God gives us what we need to accomplish God's will and purpose in the world.

At the end of Gloria Naylor's debut novel, Women of Brewster Place, the women began the arduous and seemingly impossible task of tearing down a wall that had kept them separated from the rest of the city. This group of diverse women joined hands in one action toward their liberation—it was a sign of collaborative hope. These women refused to be limited by walls—physical and emotional—so they found a way to maintain hope and to look toward a future they could shape.

Disappointments and setbacks come, but we are not to be discouraged. We work from strength to strength because God is good and God has our back. Our call is to be faithful and faith-filled—on purpose and with a purpose that is God-given and God-driven. When we are discouraged, we must hold on—a change is coming!

Step-Up: Search YouTube for videos of people whose leadership you admire. Watch them in action. Let their presentations inspire and motivate you.

Perseverance

Day: 26

Evaluating My Cup

Unless the Lord builds the house,
the builders labor in vain.
Unless the Lord watches over the city,
the guards stand watch in vain.
In vain you rise early
and stay up late,
toiling for food to eat—
for he grants sleep to those he loves.

--Psalm 127:1-2

OO OFTEN, women are asked if they can have it all—a satisfying personal life and a rewarding professional life. The typical response is that women can have it all, but not at the same time. Only women in leadership and ministry are asked about having "it" all; no one questions men about balancing life and work. It seems men can have "it" all because they have us. Male pastors can have uninterrupted sermon prep time or time to read and reflect. As women, our sermon prep time is often interrupted by the needs of others. We must serve up Sunday's sermon and have Sunday dinner ready for the family.

Too many women in ministry and leadership have bought into the superwoman syndrome. I struggle with it, too, and I think my husband really believes I have a hidden cape somewhere. Most often, out of love and not obligation, we believe that we have to be all things to all people, and we have a hard time saying "no." I most often struggle with saying no because, in the time I would take to teach you, I could have done it myself. In the time I'll take to fix your errors, I could have just done it right the first time. Sometimes we don't want to be superwoman, but life is just easier that way.

Yet, what I struggle the most with is not being superwoman to those I love. I sometimes feel forced into doing things that have nothing to do with my vision of leadership and ministry. Too often, we get caught up going along to get along. We want to be liked and seek the approval of others to make us feel better about ourselves. We justify our actions by saying we are paying our dues or that jumping through hoops is part of the process. When we look at our overloaded to-do lists, we voice a litany of reasons why we have to do what we do. We feel that if we don't do it, it won't get done. Even when we manage to say "no," we go on to explain why as if we have to justify and validate ourselves. This must stop. It has to.

Let's be clear: Superwoman is a myth. She does not exist in the real world. It is time to reassess those things to which we say "yes." It takes real wisdom to know what not to take on and what to leave behind.

"No" is a complete sentence. Try saying it without the word "but" or "because." When we say no to something, we are honoring existing commitments to which we can devote more time and ensure an excellent result. Even if we have said yes to something in the past, it does not mean we need to always say yes. We should not feel guilty about saying no; this leads to resentment, anger, and stress.

Never forget that the power to say "yes" and "no" rests with you and you alone. The voice box is yours. The lips from which the words "yes" or "no" flow are yours alone. We must stop complaining and accept full responsibility for all that is on our plates because we are the ones who loaded (or overloaded) our plates.

When you get a request to do something, take time to consider the time and energy required. Hold yourself back from saying "yes." Take a moment to ask God if this is your assignment for this season. Weigh the options; determine if the request fits your vision and mission; focus on what matters most; be honest about your answer. Can you suggest someone who might relish the opportunity to say yes to this request? Make the referral. Saying no is an important part of de-cluttering your life, relieving stress, and ensuring the effectiveness of your ministry. Learn to just say no! Give yourself this permission. You will be better because of it.

Step-Up: It may take some practice to say no to the opportunities that come your way. Stand in front of a mirror and say, "No." Say it until you mean it. If the opportunity fits with your vision and mission, sleep on it before you make a decision.

Balance

Day: 27

Grow the Gift through Grace

For God, who said, "Let light shine out of darkness," made his light shine in our hearts to give us the light of the knowledge of God's glory displayed in the face of Christ.

But we have this treasure in jars of clay to show that this all-surpassing power is from God and not from us.

--2 Corinthians 4:6-7

CHURCH USED TO BE ONE OF THE FEW PLACES people could exercise their leadership gifts. In fact, it was the place where gifts were discovered and developed. Mothers of the church—seasoned saints who had been around for a while—would often say to a child or young adult, "You have such nice handwriting. You should be a church secretary." Or "You speak so nicely. You should think about giving the announcements on Sunday morning." Or "You read the Bible so well, you should go into the ministry." Without knowing it, the mothers of the church were calling out the gifts they saw in others. Their gift of seeing the gifts in others remains priceless.

The one who received these messages were flattered and a bit nervous about claiming their gifts—they never thought of their skills as gifts. When offered the opportunity to share, they did their very best so as to not disappoint the mother who saw something in them.

We may be hard-pressed to remember the last time we received an honest and earnest compliment. Even more hard-pressed to remember when we complimented someone. We don't do the work of ministry and leadership for the accolades, but sincere compliments are great motivators for excellence.

We do better when we are appreciated and valued. The call is not to perfection; however, one's best effort is the norm. In fact, mistakes can be the springboard to excellence when we learn from them.

A water bearer in India had two large pots, each hung on each end of a pole, which he carried across his neck. One of the pots had a crack in it, and while the other pot was perfect and always delivered a full portion of water at the end of the long walk from the stream to the master's house, the cracked pot arrived only half full.

For a full two years, this went on daily, with the bearer delivering only one and a half pots full of water to his master's house.

Of course, the perfect pot was proud of its accomplishments, perfect for the end for which it was made. But the poor cracked pot was ashamed of its own imperfection and miserable that it was able to accomplish only half of what it had been made to do.

After two years of what it perceived to be a bitter failure, it spoke to the water bearer one day by the stream. "I am ashamed of myself, and I want to apologize to you."

"Why?" asked the bearer. "What are you ashamed of?"

"I have been able, for these past two years, to deliver only half my load because this crack in my side causes water to leak out all the way back to your master's house. Because of my flaws, you have to do all of this work, and you don't get full value from your efforts," the pot said.

The water bearer felt sorry for the old cracked pot, and in his compassion, he said, "As we return to the master's house, I want you to notice the beautiful flowers along the path." Indeed, as they went up the hill, the old cracked pot took notice of the sun warming the beautiful wild flowers on the side of the path, and this cheered it some.

But at the end of the trail, it still felt bad because it had leaked out half its load, and so again it apologized to the bearer for its failure. The bearer said to the pot, "Did you notice that there were flowers on your side of the path but not on the other pot's side? That's because I have always known about your flaw, and I took advantage of it. I planted flower seeds on your side of the path, and every day while we walk back from the stream, you've watered them. For two years, I have been able to pick these beautiful flowers to decorate my master's table. Without you being just the way you are, he would not have this beauty to grace his house."

Each of us has our own unique flaws. The call isn't for perfection. It is for a longing to be used in whatever way our Master sees fit. We're all cracked pots. But if we will allow it, the Lord will use all of us to be a blessing.

Step Back: Today, offer a sincere compliment to someone in your leadership or ministry circle. Send your remarks via email or text. Be specific and be honest. Then watch that team member put extra effort into his or her work.

Excellence

Day: 28

Believing in Me!

For the revelation awaits an appointed time;
it speaks of the end
and will not prove false.
Though it linger, wait for it;
it will certainly come
and will not delay.

--Habakkuk 2:3

Y SON LOVES WHEN I READ HIM The Little Engine That Could, a well-known and popular children's illustrated book. It is ranked as one of the top 100 children's books of all time. The story is about a stranded train that needs an engine to pull it over a rugged hill so that toys can be delivered to waiting boys and girls. None of the bigger engines wants to take on the task. The only offer to help comes from a small engine that is willing to try. The little engine's mantra is "I think I can, I think I can." The little engine teaches about determination, tenacity, and willpower.

Sometimes ministry feels like a stranded train—movement is stalled, obstacles are too big to navigate, setbacks come at breath-taking speed, mistakes pile up, and the vision is hidden behind stumbling blocks. We look at our vision and our reality, and all we see is a rugged mountain. We see no way to overcome the barriers in our path.

We begin to question if God is playing some cruel joke at our expense. We begin to question ourselves—do we have what it takes to achieve the call that God has placed on us? We wonder why things are so difficult for us to achieve.

Detours, delays, and denials can undermine our confidence and self-esteem. We are tempted to give in, give up, and give over our vision to someone else. We are envious of others who seem so far ahead of us. We are jealous of those who seem to have it all while we are struggling and suffering. We are intimidated by the work and sacrifice required to fulfill the vision.

Surrender and resignation are not options for women called by God. They simply aren't. God's intentions and purposes will come to fruition. We have to believe in God's call and believe in ourselves. God has given us everything we need to fulfill the vision. We have to believe we can do all things through Christ who strengthens and empowers us.

God called you on purpose and for a purpose. Your call belongs to you and only you. There is no substitute waiting in the wings if you decline the offer. Only you can accomplish what God has on your to-do list of life and ministry.

I remember a testimony given by a woman preacher. She started her ministry at a time when women were few and far apart. She didn't have immediate role models or mentors to help her. She remarked to her pastor that she was fearful because she was not a man and because her gifts paled when compared with men touted as ministerial superstars. Her pastor wisely told her that God didn't call her to be anybody else. God called her—with her gifts, graces, and flaws. She wears a silver ring as a reminder of God's presence and power. No matter where she is or what she is doing, the ring reminds her that God has her back.

God knew what God was doing in calling her and in calling us to ministry and leadership. Our path is ours to accept or reject. What God has for us is for us. No one can take that away from us. God provides all we need to achieve the vision God has given to us. We can do it!

Step Back: What tangible symbol do you have that reminds you that what God has for you is for you? Identify an item and keep it close. It might be a piece of jewelry, an item of clothing, a prayer rock, a bookmark—choose whatever speaks to your heart.

Vision

Day: 29

Follow Through

The plans of the diligent lead surely to abundance,
but everyone who is hasty comes only to want.

--Proverbs 21:5

REKKIES WILL RECOGNIZE this catch phrase: "Make it so." It is uttered by Jean-Luc Picard, a character in Star Trek and the captain of the USS Enterprise-D and the Enterprise-E, giving permission for a subordinate to execute an order.

We can have the blueprints, building permits, construction materials, and general contractors in place, but the building won't go up until someone starts the work. The same is true for ministry and mission.

We must follow-through and get going. Why take the time to grasp the vision, mobilize people, and gather resources if we're not going to actually do the work? I've found that many churches don't have a strategic plan, and if they do, it's sitting on a shelf somewhere and has not been used. So many visions fail to get off the ground because we are overwhelmed or too tired to get going. We get addicted to planning and forget that the whole point of planning is to reach a goal or build a building or get a ministry going.

I remember when my son was born. All of these items came to my home. The outside of the boxes showed wonderful products that could help us and make our lives better. Yet, nearly every box shared a similar statement, "Some assembly required." No matter how great they looked on the outside, they challenged me to do the work of putting them together. Each came with a book of instructions. The parts were randomly packaged. The steps to taking all the items in the box and transferring them into the image on the box were numbered. I had to follow the instructions, or I would have never been able to maximize the gift.

It's time to no longer be consumed with marketing the vision or even talking about the vision. We cast the vision long ago. Now it is time to move the vision forward by any means necessary.

Time and time again, I've seen way too many women make the vision look great on paper, and yet, it stays there indefinitely. When will you take the necessary steps, do the hard work of ensuring that what God has shown you shall be? Too many people feel that writing the vision is planting the seed and all they must do is wait for the harvest. Not so! We are called to cultivate the seed for it to grow with water, light, pruning, and care. No growth happens with procrastination. It doesn't happen with PowerPoints and marking pens. It only happens with action and hard work. It doesn't happen just because you want it. Vision becomes reality because you do what is necessary. Follow God's instructions to bring the vision to life. Remember that some assembly is required on your part. God has delivered the necessary pieces to you. Now put it together.

We must be intentional about following the steps and instructions —do what God is requiring of you. Each day I determine I will get at least one or two things accomplished. I list them out along with the necessary steps I must take to feel a sense of accomplishment by the end of the day. Most days, I have made it so. Every once in a while, I must leave a task until the following day. Yet I am clear that God believes in me. In other words, today is your day to "Make it so!"

Step Back: What is one concrete thing you can do today to move your vision forward? Do you need to find a resource or call someone or pay someone? Decide what step you can take TODAY and do it!

Strategy

Day: 30

Hand Me Oxygen

Finally, be strong in the Lord and in his mighty power. Put on the full armor of God, so that you can take your stand against the devil's schemes. For our struggle is not against flesh and blood, but against the rulers, against the authorities, against the powers of this dark world and against the spiritual forces of evil in the heavenly realms. Therefore put on the full armor of God, so that when the day of evil comes, you may be able to stand your ground, and after you have done everything, to stand. Stand firm then, with the belt of truth buckled around your waist, with the breastplate of righteousness in place, and with your feet fitted with the readiness that comes from the gospel of peace. In addition to all this, take up the shield of faith, with which you can extinguish all the flaming arrows of the evil one. Take the helmet of salvation and the sword of the Spirit, which is the word of God.
And pray in the Spirit on all occasions with all kinds of prayers and requests. With this in mind, be alert and always keep on praying for all the Lord's people.

--Ephesians 6:10-18

*D*ENVER IS KNOWN AS The Mile High City because its elevation is exactly one mile above sea level. The air is thinner and drier. It is said that golf balls go ten times faster because of the atmospheric pressure. It is important that one allows the body to adjust to the change. The Denver Chamber of Commerce suggests that visitors: drink lots of water, eat foods rich in potassium to balance electrolytes, monitor physical exercise because the effects are more intense, and make sure to have sunscreen and sunglasses because there is 25 percent less protection from the sun. They offer these suggestions to make people's stay in Denver safe and enjoyable.

Don't you wish ministry and leadership came with similar instructions and suggestions? Instead, it is left up to us to determine how to best take care of ourselves as we tackle our to-do lists. I can tell you this: It will take wisdom.

We will never have stress-free lives; stress is part of being human. When God is your boss and the vision is tangible, stress is natural. We want to give our best to a God who gave all on Calvary's cross. We will naturally have times of high stress and times when we have to push through that to-do list. However, it is imperative that we build downtime into our schedules.

We need Sabbath time in order to renew, refresh, and refuel for the leadership and ministry tasks that are required. Sabbath can include prayer, meditation, a gratitude log—whatever feeds your spirit and soul.

Sabbath and pampering ourselves go hand-in-hand. Pampering is a not a selfish act. Taking care of our bodies on the outside is essential for internal health and well-being. It is well worth the effort and expense to develop a wellness regimen. You will need to be consistent with your regimen—you'll have something to look forward to when things are overwhelming.

What downtime has done for me is to assist me in hearing what God is calling me to do very specifically. It is not enough to love God and not listen to His daily commands regarding our call to ministry. Some days we are called to work, and other days we are called to rest. However, if we aren't carving out the time to listen to God's command, we will miss the vision God is trying to make into a reality in our lives.

A young boy by the name of James had a desire to be the most famous manufacturer and salesman of cheese in the world. He planned on becoming rich and famous by making and selling cheese, and he began with a little buggy pulled by a pony named Paddy. After making his cheese, he would load his wagon, and he and Paddy would drive down the streets of Chicago to sell the cheese. As the months passed, the young boy began to despair because he was not making any money, in spite of his long hours and hard work.

One day he pulled his pony to a stop and began to talk to him. He said, "Paddy, there is something wrong. We are not doing it right. I am afraid we have things turned around, and our priorities are not where they ought to be. Maybe we ought to serve God and place Him first in our lives." The boy drove home and made a covenant that, for the rest of his life, he would first serve God and then would work as God directed.

Many years after this, the young boy, now a man, stood as Sunday School Superintendent at North Shore Baptist Church in Chicago and said, "I would rather be a layman in the North Shore Baptist Church than to head the greatest corporation in America. My first job is serving Jesus."

So, every time you take a take a bite of Philadelphia cream cheese, sip a cup of Maxwell House, mix a quart of Kool-Aid, slice up a DiGiorno pizza, cook a pot of Kraft macaroni & cheese, spread some Grey Poupon, stir a bowl of Cream of Wheat, slurp down some Jell-O, eat the cream out of the middle of an Oreo cookie, or serve some Stove Top, remember a boy, his pony named Paddy, and the promise little James L. Kraft made to serve God and work as He directed.

Mr. Kraft was able to bring forth an empire, over time, because he let God direct him. I am pretty sure that in his quiet moments, his Sabbath rest, he gained clarity about his call.

God longs to direct us just the same. God wants to give you and me very clear instructions about how to bring this vision into reality. We cannot quit. What we can do is stop to take a breath and get clear directions. You can get to the mountain top, over time, when you take in the air.

Step Back: Go with God's direction. You cannot go wrong. Remember that all work and no play leads to burn-out. Step back and let God direct your path. Make a pampering appointment today—book that massage, get that manicure and pedicure, visit the make-up counter and get a make-over. Better yet, call up some girlfriends and make it a girl's day, afternoon, or night out!

A Final Thought...

Bloom Where You are Planted

Therefore, since we are surrounded by such a great
cloud of witnesses, let us throw off everything that
hinders and the sin that so easily entangles. And let
us run with perseverance the race marked out for
us, fixing our eyes on Jesus, the pioneer and
perfecter of faith. For the joy set before him he
endured the cross, scorning its shame, and sat down
at the right hand of the throne of God. Consider
him who endured such opposition from sinners, so
that you will not grow weary and lose heart.

--Hebrews 12:1-3

WE HAVE HEARD THIS SO MANY TIMES that we barely pay much attention anymore: "Bloom where you are planted." The sentiment has the marks of resignation and surrender to adverse circumstances or situations. We may believe that we are destined to be in a place that is not our choice. We may feel that being in that place is our cross to bear. There is no joy there, no happiness, and, more importantly, no way out.

I get into so much trouble when I offer this as a prayer—before I can explain, the eyes roll, the lips curl up, and I can see the "blah-blah-blah, yada-yada-yada" forming on people's lips.

Think about it—some plants will never bloom where they are planted because the soil is too alkaline or too acidic; there is too

123

much sunlight or not enough sunlight; the soil is too dry or too wet. Plants need optimal conditions in which to bloom and thrive. They will wilt or bloom according to the conditions.

The key to whether we bloom or wilt is whether we are planted in the right place. If we find ourselves in places that are too dry or shady, we will wither and die. We must believe that God has placed us where we are for a purpose. There is a difference between being placed by God and placing ourselves. We think we know better than God and sometimes find ourselves in hard places.

I look at the church where I serve. The building was destroyed by fire just six months before I arrived. The congregation of forty people, most of them retired, did nearly everything on Sunday, from worship to fellowship, to monthly meetings and more. I am clear that God gave me an anointing for this particular church. We are nothing like we were the day I arrived. In fact, this church had been known as a clergy killer. However, the answer from God when I prayed was, "Go and I will be with you." I went, not because I wanted to go there. I was happy at the tiny church where I was serving. Yet the call of God was clear. God gave me an anointing for my assignment.

When God does the planting, we are assured that we will bloom, no matter what. We begin by appreciating where we are. All we have to do is remember from whence we've come—look back over your journey and see how far God has brought you.

We acknowledge our companions along our journeys—family, friends, and colleagues who keep us warm. We spend time with them and nurture these relationships.

Blooming requires focusing on the big picture of God's intentions and purposes and our calling to co-create God's kingdom here on earth. Blooming requires balance, excellence, vision, strategy, and perseverance.

Blooming means we learn to go with the flow—not in a passive, resigned manner, but rather with energy and gratitude for being chosen by God for such a time as this.

There is an old saying that is appropriate here: The grass may be greener on the other side of the fence, but it still needs to be mowed!

Let us thank God that we have been called, chosen, and planted. Now, let us bloom!

One Last Step: Start a Gratitude Jar, a clear container is preferred. Decorate it as you wish or have others in your support circle help decorate it. Keep a supply of post-it notes or colorful slips of paper and pens nearby. Each day or several times a day, write down what you are grateful for and add these notes to your jar. Place the jar in a prominent place where you will see it regularly. The jar will be a visual reminder that life is filled with wonderful things.

A Final Thought...

About the Author

www.TeamJenkins.org

A VISIONARY PASTOR AND TEACHER representing a new generation of leaders, Rev. Courtney Clayton Jenkins serves as the Senior Pastor and Teacher of South Euclid United Church of Christ (formerly Euclid Avenue Congregational Church). At the age of 27, Rev. Jenkins made history when she became the first woman, first African American and the youngest pastor called to lead this special congregation. Since that day in 2010, Rev. Jenkins has led the multi-cultural, multi-generational, inner-city congregation to become the vibrant church that it is today, but first she had to lead it out of the ashes.

Just six months before Rev. Jenkins was asked to serve, the historic church was struck by lightning and the architectural gem was completely destroyed by fire. With courage, the congregation called the young and dynamic "hip-hop" preacher to become their pastor to allow God to do "a new thing."

That "new thing" happened to be nothing short of a transformation. Under Rev. Jenkins' leadership, the congregation adopted a new strategic plan for revitalization and a clarified mission for outreach, which includes innovative ways to use technology to do God's work. Now in a new location and with a new name, the church is experiencing exponential growth and a revived passion for serving humanity through ministry and mission. In the midst of a growing congregation, Rev. Jenkins is currently overseeing a $8.15 million construction project for the campus of South Euclid.

Born and raised in Cleveland Ohio, Rev. Jenkins holds a Masters of Divinity from Princeton Theological Seminary with a concentration in Preaching and Congregational Ministry. She earned a Bachelor of Arts in English Literature from Spelman College.

In the United Church of Christ denomination, Rev. Jenkins is an ordained minister and serves in several capacities. Previously, she served as the Designated Pastor of Shaker Heights Community Church, United Church of Christ. She is the first woman to be ordained at the historic Mt. Zion Congregational Church in Cleveland.

Rev. Jenkins is Co-Founder of the *Without Walls Ministry, a* retreat designed to glorify God and edify women in ministry. She has served on numerous boards and committees of local and national ecumenical organizations.

Rev. Jenkins is married to her seminary sweetheart, Rev. Cory C. Jenkins, Senior Pastor of the Shiloh Baptist Church, which is also one of the oldest congregations in Cleveland. They travel the country as a team facilitating workshops and seminars on family stabilization. On March 18, 2014, they rejoiced in the arrival of their son, Caleb, who is their "gift from God!" They are excited about this new chapter in their lives as they continue on the path of love and ministry together.

In January 2012, Cleveland Magazine selected Rev. Cory and Rev. Courtney as one of the "Most Interesting Couples." In July of the same year, they were featured by Black Enterprise Magazine as a new paradigm for careers in faith.

Rev. Jenkins is committed to and humbled by God's calling and purpose upon her life. As she joyfully leads her congregation in serving God, she continues to pursue discipleship well beyond its walls to find new ways for the next generation to impact this nation with His unconditional love and almighty power.